"Do I visit San Francisco to see the sights? the views? the restaurants? the Golden Gate? No, I come to visit the cafes, drink the coffee and wander the neighborhoods "

Sara Perry, author, "The New Complete Coffee Book," Chronicle

"THE CAFES OF SAN FRANCISCO celebrates these treasures ... and enlisted the aid of some big names in putting together this pretty book."

Debby Morse, San Francisco Examiner

"Indispensible when you need that Paris 'fix'. Lists toutes! If you seek a sanctuary, the interior an old zinc counter and worn leather banquettes rescued from a Les Halles cafe, you need this guide. Only the smoke from Gauloise is missing."

Cara Black, author of "Murder in the Sentier"

"FOUR AND A HALF STARS!" "I was immediately drawn by photos of some of my favorite cafes...the book makes me want to go out and explore San Francisco's cafes."

Martha Bakerjian, About.com / Sanfrancisco.about.com

"Both the photography and general layout of this book are catchy"

Cory O'Malley, Metro.Pop Magazine

"THE CAFES OF SAN FRANCISCO is a delicious new book, packed full of lots of information and lots of ... photos. Best of all it introduces you to these intriguing cafes of the San Francisco Bay Area."

Narsai David, KCBS Food & Wine Editor

"This lovingly photographed guide captures the welcoming essence of cafe life: that perfect combination of bohemian spirit and intellectual buzz."

Andrea Hanis, Travel Editor, Chicago Sun-Times

"When it comes to cafes, San Francisco has one of the richest and most diverse traditions in the United States. The book winds through the neighborhoods of San Francisco and communities like the North Bay and Berkeley, giving a snapshot of cafe culture and history along the way."

Anita MacAuley, Fresh Cup Magazine, www.freshcup.com

"After reviewing a copy of this book, I wanted to spread the word about how incredible it is. If you live in SF and have ever been to any of its coffee houses, I highly recommend picking up a copy of THE CAFES OF SAN FRANCISCO."

Tamar Love, Literary Arts Editor, SF Station, www.sfstation.com

When cafe life thrives, talk is a shared limberness of the mind that improves appetite for conversation: an adequate sentence maker is then made good, a good one excellent, an excellent one extraordinary.

Vivian Gornick

Interior of a cafe in North Beach, 1967, Photograph by Mary Anne Kramer

San Francisco is no exception to the rule that there is something distinctive about every city that is a city. With its gay bohemian life, excellent cafes, bright lights and real people, San Francisco is known in every corner of the United States and most parts of the world for its distinctive way of doing things, and particularly its way of enjoying life.

15 January 1919
San Francisco Chronicle

Cafes are considered the ideal meeting places both in San Francisco and in Italy. Italians actually played a very important role in the development of San Francisco. We can easily say that many of the qualities that are considered typical of San Francisco, such as open-mindedness, appreciation for good food and good wine, opera, art and the humanities, in other words the love of beauty classically interpreted as balance, are also found in Italian culture and society. San Francisco culture is unique in many different ways. Let me just say that, in general, cities that love cafes, especially outdoor cafes, tend to be livelier and more welcoming than those where cafe life is not so widespread.

Francesco Sciortino
Consul General of Italy, San Francisco

Bartenders pouring the Buena Vista Cafe's famous Irish Coffees

CAFE REVIEWS: A.K. CRUMP

OTHER TEXT: KRISTEN JENSEN, P SEGAL

PROOFREADING: STEPHANIE G. CRUMP, RANDY GREEN

ORIGINAL COVER DESIGN: HEATHER MCDONALD (MCDONALD DESIGN)

DESIGN CONSULTANTS: AKIRA BRYSON, RANDY GREEN, RONALD MARGULIS & PATRICIA PAUL (RAM COMMUNICATIONS), HEATHER MCDONALD (MCDONALD DESIGN)

PHOTO CREDITS: LISA KNUTSON PHOTOGRAPHY (MARIN CAFES); RICHARD BARNES (SFMOMA); ARLEEN NG (BUZZ 9); GEORGE BROOKE (VESUVIO); MARY ANNE KRAMER (1967 NORTH BEACH CAFE); RICHARD GROSS (NIEBAUM-COPPOLA), STEPHANIE RAUSSER (CUPS MAGAZINE), PALM PICTURES (GIGI); OTHER PHOTOGRAPHS COURTESY OF TCB-CAFE PUBLISHING, CAFE SOCIETY, TULLY'S COFFEE, PEET'S COFFEE & TEA, CAFFE TRINITY, SOUTH BEACH CAFE, SAN FRANCISCO LIBRARY HISTORICAL PHOTOGRAPH COLLECTION, ILLY COFFEE, BALBOA CAFE, PLUMPJACK CAFE, TORANI, SAN FRANCISCO ART INSTITUTE, SAN FRANCISCO ZOO, SCHARFFEN BERGER CHOCOLATE MAKER, ZHENA'S GYPSY TEA, DAVID RIO TEA, STONESTREET WINES, SAMOVAR TEA LOUNGE

MANY THANKS ARE DUE TO MAYOR WILLIAM L. BROWN JR., JOEY ALTMAN, FRANCIS FORD COPPOLA, CONSUL GENERAL OF ITALY FRANCESCO SCIORTINO, COLMAN ANDREWS, JOHN MARIANI, CHRIS RUBIN, WILL DURST, GARY RULLI, BARBARA GRAVES, RUTH WEISS, SPENCER CHRISTIAN, JOHN MARKS, MICHEL RICHARD, MICHAEL KRAUS, DAN STORPER, MICHAEL SMUIN, JOAN OSBURN, NEAL MORGAN, PHIL FRANK, JACK DAVIS, JAIME CORTEZ, ERICA HESS, CELANIE FRESH, PETER JARIT, BAR ARCHITECTS, DIANA BARRAND, RIKO KNIGHT, KIM NOVAK, MATTHEW BLAIR, MERLA ZELLERBACH, JANE.ORG, KRISTI DECAMINADA, JENNIFER FRENCH, DEBORAH BERMAN, DAVID LATIMER, PETRA SCHUMANN, JOHNNY DAVIS, BILL RODDY, TAJ DHILLON, CONCEICAO DAMASCENO, TRINA ROBBINS, PAMELA FISHMAN, CELENA HODKINS, LAURIE ARMSTRONG, ALEXANDRA RUNDEL, SUSAN HEWITT, ELIZABETH ASHFORD, GRACEANNWALDEN, ELAINE SOSA, CESAR CALLAO, QUINTAN ANA WIKSWO, ROSEMARY FURFARO, GEORGIA PETERSON DE MACHUCA, ROBERT GREEN, CHANDLER CRUMP, ANISE CRUMP, CHARLES GATEWOOD, DAVID UNGER, CATALINA BAJENARU, ELIZABETH STROUD, VALENCIA CHOCOLATES, SANTIAGO RODRIGUEZ, STACY COOPER DENT

tcb-cafe publishing

PO BOX 471706
SAN FRANCISCO, CALIFORNIA 94147
USA

THE CAFES OF SAN FRANCISCO

3rd Edition

Contents

About this Guide

What is a Cafe Guidebook? According to the American Heritage Dictionary, a guidebook is "a handbook of directions and other information, especially for travelers or tourists." That's the definition we used for this series of Cafe Guides. It's a fun & delicious discovery tour of various cafes across the San Francisco Bay Area for residents and travelers.

Regional in Focus: The cafe scene is regional in flavor. Some San Francisco Bay Area regions have an older cafe tradition than others, and that affects the types of cafes for which they are known. The type of weather that a region experiences also may influence the outdoor seating available, and when it can be used.

The author and editors try to give you a feel for these regional differences by dividing the Bay Area into three major areas: San Francisco by neighborhood, the North Bay, and the East & South Bay.

Profiles: This Cafe Guide provides profiles of selected cafes in each region. In general we try to stay away from critical reviews of the cafes, or things like the quality of their coffee or whether they have wi-fi access (too changeable), simply because that is not the purpose of this guidebook. One person's delight might be another's fright. There are however a number of expert sources for readers who would like to access ratings and reviews of cafes. There is also our favorite source for regional customer reviews: Yelp.com.

Representational: Great cafes are always subjective, and should always be fun. There is no one-size-fits-all cafe for the cafe lovers of the world. This guidebook is therefore a subjective selection of cafes in each region that the editors believe represent some of the interesting and delicious choices that you might find. New cafes arrive on the scene each month, and existing ones continue to evolve, which means that an exhaustive compendium of them in print could never be complete (and would be way more than 160+ pages). If we did not include your favorite cafe in a particular region, let us know. Perhaps we'll include them in a future Edition.

ENJOY!

Just as in Paris, Vienna, and Rome, the cafes of San Francisco play a large role in our daily lives, as well as in the itineraries of our visitors. And why shouldn't they, when so many ground-breaking ideas and cuisines have emerged from their premises. San Francisco has always been a town where people gather information, think about the facts, and provide informed opinions on a variety of topics. The topics can range from politics to music, from art to the environment, from literature to tribal philosophies. It doesn't matter, because we have thoughtful opinions on any subject.

At its heart, to be a San Franciscan is to be connected to the world around you, and our cafes have always played a key role in being a major forum for discourse. This is why San Francisco has always seemed to be several years, if not decades, ahead of its time.

A.K. Crump, Author

San Francisco

is a café kind of town. There are hundreds of them, catering to every walk of life. From the bohemians of North Beach to the underground artists of the Mission district to the suits in the Financial district. It seems that every segment of society in San Francisco cherishes their local java joint.

What these "caterers of caffeine" have in common is that they are really neighborhood sanctuaries. Many of them have all the comforts that you would find at a well-stocked friend's house: coffee, tea, bagels, and depending on what part of the city you are in, freshly-prepared foods ranging from Mediterranean to New Age-Vegan to Russian. You can find newspapers, periodicals and a variety of other publications in a multitude of languages, usually representing the demographics within a five-block radius. You may even find games that friends amd strangers can challenge each other to, all the while sipping belly-warming beverages and couch-grooving to funky world-beat tunes.

But make no mistake, this is how it is to be within a community. What you see is where you live. The café is where you can really get to know your neighbor, and where you will probably meet the person who can give you the Italian or guitar lessons you've always wanted.

These are the "dining rooms" that most of our small apartments don't have, and they provide a special sort of restoration.

Let the rest of the world have the cookie-cutter coffeehouse chains with their deli-cases of mass produced overly sweet breakfast pastries. I'll take the tuna melt on a sesame seed bagel from One World Cafe, or the Middle Eastern pistachio and honey filo triangles from Café Abir, or anything from Citizen Cake any day of the week.

And as the times change so do the cafés. Even though many of them have a retro-sixties sort of feel, there always seems to be something topical and edgy about them. It's sometimes found hung on the walls, oozing from the speakers or blaring from the mouths of local poets and storytellers. These are places that you go when you want to be in touch with the people you live among.

So if you want to know your community, put down the newspaper Society Page, and go to your corner coffeehouse and be a part of it.

Chef Joey Altman,
"Bay Cafe" television host

I think our love of cafés in San Francisco really speaks to the area's unique and diverse history.

It grew out of the counter-culture movement where ideas were passionately debated and exchanged in café settings and it reflects the rich ethnic diversity that allows us to experience tastes and cultures from every corner of the world in our own backyard. The strong presence of our large Asian community has given us a long appreciation of Eastern philosophies and exposure to a rich abundance of teas, herbs, history and ceremony, all of which are also captured by the café culture. It really is a vibrant, romantic and eclectic sub-culture all its own, unparalleled by any other place in the world. To appreciate the café culture of San Francisco is to embrace what I refer to as "Sip by Sip living" -- the slowing down and savoring of each moment.

Barbara Graves
Minister of Commerce
The Republic of Tea

Home

to some of the world's most renowned chefs, enterprising businesspeople, innovative musicians and cutting-edge authors, San Francisco has always attracted the brightest and most creative minds. As with any other cosmopolitan city, our propensity towards creativity and diversity is partially due to our unique cafe culture.

Neighborhood cafes are like a second home to many San Franciscans. During the weekend, you can see café patrons reading the latest novel, typing away on a laptop, partaking in high-spirited discussions or simply enjoying an espresso. Just as there are a plethora of coffee drinks to suit the diverse palates of coffee drinkers, there are a variety of cafes for San Franciscans and visitors alike to enjoy. Some patronize cafes in North Beach, sipping cappuccinos where Beat writers Ginsberg and Kerouac once sat, while others prefer to perch themselves at an outdoor café and watch the unique parade of San Franciscans pass by.

Whatever your preference, you are almost guaranteed a good conversation and a cup of some of the world's best coffee.

Willie L. Brown, Jr., former Mayor of San Francisco

The thing

about San Francisco that I love is that the neighborhoods ARE distinct from each other so when you go from one to the other, it's as if you are in an entirely different city, or country for that matter, except each area is populated by open, interesting individuals.

Phil Frank
Cartoonist ("Farley")
and Social Observer

In my mind

and heart, it is not just the sights and museums that capture the essence of a city or village, but rather the life of the cafes. The cafe is a gathering place, to see and be seen as well as a refuge where one can be alone without the interruptions and pressures of everyday life. Historically, it is where artists, writers, performers, politicians, traders and the peuple met and cross fertilized their ideas & schemes and so it is about culture, change, civilization and revolution, as well as coffee and wine.

What makes cafe society, cafe society is that it is inclusive- open to all that love the cafe life. In France, the cafe is the "third place," apart from work and home, where one can put time on hold and just be who you are. San Francisco cafe society, is in the authentic European tradition and so has become a meeting place for the creatives of a myriad of arts and technology movements as well as the epicenter for cross fertilization of art and technology.

Joan Osburn
Cafe Society

It has always

been my dream to be part of an artistic 'critical mass,' in which artists and thinkers share their ideas, stimulate each other while also enjoying a bohemian atmosphere. My cafe is located right in the middle of what used to be known at the turn of the century as 'the Latin Quarter' of San Francisco. I spend my happiest moments there, sitting at a table outside in the corner, looking across the street at the laundry hanging out of the windows.

Francis Ford Copppola
filmmaker

The Cafe Lifestyle

Throughout centuries of civilization, differing somewhat from culture to culture, one thing stands out as a well-beloved institution, and that is the café experience. The café, pub, coffee house, inn is the meeting-place for a community, a social interaction over the beverage of choice, a moment of relaxation for everyone except those behind the bar, a chance to greet known companions or meet intriguing newcomers. Some cafés, by the nature of their clientele, become famous as centers of the arts.

For a decade of my adult life, I lived in North Beach, that once-bohemian heart of San Francisco, immersed in the total café existence. The first hours of the day were spent in the Caffé Trieste, where my father had been a regular when it opened in the '50s, a piece of his old country where he could speak his language, discuss poetry and politics, and have a decent espresso. In the family tradition, I began the day there downing a few lattes, catching up on all the neighborhood gossip, chatting with friends, or, when left to my own devices, working on whatever writing I needed to complete. Late in the afternoon, or early evening, I walked up the street to the front patio of the Savoy Tivoli, where most evenings passed amicably with conversation, and the amusement of neighborhood slag-fests, and martinis, watching the parade of humanity on the street. The Savoy had a huge crowd of regulars who, like me, knew just about everybody on the terrace, sometimes all too well; any newcomer to our living room was met, purposefully, by someone among us, and discussed by all the hopeless wags. Other topics to get a lot of play: what we were writing, what other people were writing, what we were reading, and the characteristics and suitable fates of the cohabitors of this café planet. I never found this boring, and on the nights when I was forced to leave the neighborhood, I found myself wondering what I had missed at the Savoy. Fortunately I would hear multiple versions of what happened over the next day's wake-up latte, daily café Rashomon.

One never knew when there'd be a new entertainment on the street in front of the Savoy. One summer, a 20-piece French brass band would pull up their bus, bring out their instruments and play for us every few weeks, and we loved them. For years we had occasional performances by an amazing fellow, a son, one guessed, of some Caribbean plantation magnate. His immense white limo would pull up, he would leap from the back and this ebony prince in his immaculate white suit and white straw fedora would bellow arias from Italian opera. It was awful, but when he was gone, everybody was in a much better mood. Or

perhaps, one of the grand beat poet survivors would show up and have a raging argument with someone else, a prime topic for weeks of discussion.

Every so often you'd leave your seat on the terrace, and go inside to the bar to talk to Franco, the bartender and Buddha of the Beach, perhaps sit down to have a round with that trustfund baby who burned out with the postwar bohemian expatriots, and knew Durrell, His Lord and Lady Leslie, or my dear friend and primary cruising partner, O'Toole, who had come to Franco's presence. Or you might stroll out with a few friends to get dinner somewhere, or to go by a few other places, in search of a someone you might want to see, who'd be hiding in another café, working on his screenplay. You'd go by the Roma, saunter through to the back garden, and back out again, then up to the garden behind the original Old Spaghetti Factory, and see who was contributing to the night air beneath the fig and datura trees, peek into the Trieste. You'd walk into places, scan the clientele, and failing to find the person you sought, head back out to look in more unsociable spots. The truly retiring would be sequestered at a table upstairs at the Europa on Columbus, or upstairs at Vesuvio.

Once in a while you'd run into someone else along the way, stop and have a something, but eventually you'd be back at the Savoy. And if you waited long enough on the terrace, the person you were looking for would at least saunter by. Sitting on the terrace, Jack Sarfatti would tell you about his newest theory, his personal war with a huge figure in New Age big business, or books, or you'd nod at the funny rants of Kim, whose first claim to fame was being the subject of an article in Esquire, about golden boys who have surprised everyone by not being famous yet. Stephen Schwartz would come in with plenty to say, about his current book or this week's attempted assassination of his character. My beloved pal Miss X taught me everything I know about neurosis. Lin, Danise, Pamela and Miss X became sisters I never had. Dozens of others offered great company while you waited for a particular person to show up.

Writers often have some affinity to cafés. Their work precludes co-workers, being a solitary endeavor, but the loneliness is tempered by the presence of other bodies. The voices you choose to tune in tell you stories, give you plots, or give you, with observation, the details with which your characters are adorned, patterns of speech, expressions, garments, body language. I wrote a book in those naughty days called Caffé Chiachiarino (Caffé Little Blabbermouth) based entirely on stories people told me over drinks. I didn't do it well enough, but it sits there, in one of my filing cabinets, perhaps material for the days when I give up society and retire to a cork-lined room.

In retrospect, those years were like a minor golden era in the history of café life. A true golden era arose in Paris during the life of Proust, and perhaps partly because of him, as he was a café habitué, one of those people who, if you sat down beside him in a café, would say something witty; surely his appearances were discussed by others who saw him after he was gone. His friend Léon Daudet, in his book Salons et journaux, remembers the charm of café nights with Proust, "...wrapped up in woolens like a Chinese knick-knack. He would ask for a grappa de raisin and a glass of water and declare that he just got up, that he had influenza, that he was going back to bed, that the noise was bothering him, glance around him anxiously, then mockingly, finally bursting out in a magical laughter and stay. Soon coming from his lips, hastily and tentatively offered, remarks of extraordinary originality and perceptions of diabolical subtlety..."

When Proust rose from bed in the late evening, without a particular social occasion to rouse him, he often went for a cruise of the cafés. Like most café afficianados, Proust had his favorites; he was most inclined to go to Larue's or the Café Weber, or to dine at the ultrachic Ritz, all places of sumptuous quality where the well-to-do gathered to eat, drink and socialize. The Ritz became something of a second home, thanks, no doubt, to his habit of tipping extravagantly. Long after the Ritz had closed for the night, Proust could send one of his household to fetch him a beer there, as they'd been shown and permitted access to the supply in the wee hours.

In the book Toulouse-Lautrec's Table, yet another glorious work in the series that gave us Dining With Proust, and co-created by one of the Proust volume's collaborators, Jean-Bernard Naudin, we are told of the scene at the Café Weber. Regulars included Robert de Montesquiou, that likely model for Charlus, and definite model for Whistler's portrait, Léon Daudet, Debussy, Colette's husband Willy, and certainly Lautrec himself. Proust frequently dined there, according to his biographers, but sometimes, in the time-honored tradition of cruising café society, "... the collar of his coat half turned-up, his pockets stuffed with magazines and books, ever looking for someone he never found, Marcel Proust would make his appearance... then retrace his steps, push through the door, and vanish."

Certainly Proust must have made similar appearances

at the Bar du Pont-Royale, next door to his publishers, Gallimard. This house, started by a partnership of three that included André Gide, had rejected him at first (as told in PST #4) but later had a change of heart, and all their editors and writers met there to do after-hours business or just drink. Considering Proust's nocturnal schedule, what better place for him to confer with his editors?

Is it possible that he never cruised the Flore, where Huysmans (the other writer who seemed to find inspiration from de Montesquiou) and the Surrealists hung out, Aux Deux Maggots, where Oscar Wilde drank twice each day, and the menu bears the motto "Rendez-vous de l'élite intellectuel" or the Brasserie Lipp, the other headquartes of Nouvelle Revue Francaise/ Gallimard? Proust left such a mass of minutia about his life in his correspondence that we are inclined to think that we can account for every minute; in fact we can't, and I dare say that many of his unexplained moments out of the house were spent looking for the right company in Paris cafés.

Proust's café life was to outlive his terrestrial one. After his death, at the Café de l'Arrivée, Samuel Beckett went to avoid the company of other writers, and there wrote Proust in 1931.

All my adult life I have known that my true calling, the one way that I would make my fortune, so I might some day sit down at ease and simply write, would be to own the greatest café on earth, or the greatest cafés, as I plan to open them in all my favorite cities

"The joy of those who made their way into the cafes was the greater... the client ordered a drink and the waiter hurried off to get it. Then, while he waited for it to come, keeping his eyes glued to each fresh arrival, longing to start a conversation with him... while those present were drinking and playing and keeping up a continuous flow of gay talk... careless ease and a general sense of well-being..."

-Jean Santeuil

in the world. My café would be as much a salon as anything else, not filled with a decor chosen by some cutting edge designer, but filled with fine art, with books, great music, the thousands of extraordinary people I have met, the thousands I have yet to meet and, of course, the HQ of The Marcel Proust Support Group.

I have come very close many times in my life to getting what I want. Through each near-miss, besides suffering a certain unavoidable disappointment, I have learned an amazing amount about the hard edges, pitfalls and disasters of business. Savvy now, after eleven years in my own catering business and the knocks sustained in my effort to escape this dreadful career, which frequently demands stretches of 18-hour days on one's feet, I continue to insist on the hard way out: my café will be the creation of my life, it will be me, and so I must own most of the shares in it, and I continue to search for solely financial investors.

The beloved Dean Gustafson, who knows me very well, and keeps a close eye on my business prospects, came up with an idea the other night as we looked over the sketches of Paris for this issue. "Thousands of people read Proust Said That," he said, "the kind of people who are drawn to you, your values, and what you have to say... So you should write an article about cafés, and tell them what you are looking for, and maybe the right investors will show up."

There was something about this idea that was so delightful; my efforts to reach investors have been, so far, through all the usual channels, addressing persons of business who have a keen eye for the bottom line on their p and l's, but no obsession to create, and profit by, the Aux Deux Maggots of the century. They might see the value of a chain that features the souveniers of pop music, but few of these people understand, because they probably don't read themselves, the utter beauty of books, or the attraction that such a place would have for a population starved for a literary milieu.

Dozens of potential investors have surfaced over the last few years. "We're VERY interested," they tell me, "Let's have lunch." Or my young friend, the venture capital broker, will turn up a prospect who, for nearly a year, will propose investing a fifth of the needed capital, demanding this or that explanation of a detail of the estimated costs, and holding me at bay while his accountants ponder the prospects. When I decided that one such person was a wash-out, he came back with the offer of the total investment, dangling the Big Carrot while his accountants spent another long stretch of months convincing him he was crazy, or perhaps he was just enjoying the power of making me crazy. In theory there are half a dozen people out there who have the all the needed money and are willing to invest it; I have yet to see a single dime.

Recently I have considered the ways in which other cultures deal with the investment situation. In San Francisco's Chinese and Korean communities, I hear, groups of people will contribute small sums to the big picture, and open business even though no one has more than a few thousand dollars. "Hmmm," I say, "A hundred people with a few thousand dollars

"My numerous dinners at restaurants have made my stomach good as new. I eat much more there, however, but much more slowly. Besides, eating at restaurants is my substitute for Evian, and going away, and holidays in the country. Anyhow, everyone thinks I'm looking very well."

-Letter to his mother, August, 1902

each would provide the funding for the cafe of my dreams, and I believe, of theirs, with half of their dollars stowed in the bank collecting interest, facilitating repayment."

Anyone who knows business realizes that opening without reserves in the bank is foolhardy; you must have resources to pay the bills until you have developed your clientele. Such a person wouldn't trust anyone who opened a business without back-up funds in the budget, plans of an amateur. So I look for twice what I really need, a stack of executive summaries waits in my office, and beyond them, the pile of blah-blah business plans. Perhaps you might like one.

P Segal

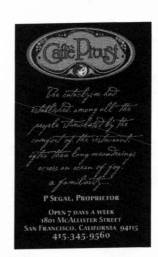

Coffee is good for talent, but genius wants prayer.

Ralph Waldo Emerson

Jean Renoir
once remarked that "All great civilizations are based on loitering", and the genuine cafe experience involves exactly that: hanging around aimlessly. The coffee or tea or drinks or pastries are an excuse to occupy the chair, and to watch the passing parade, and to talk or not talk, scribble or sketch or not scribble or sketch. Real cafes are places where you can sit for as long as you want and do nothing-at least nothing that people realize you're doing.

Colman Andrews
Editor-in-Chief
SAVEUR

Everyone should have a favorite cafe, if only to fall in and out of love.

John Mariani, ESQUIRE Magazine

North Beach & Downtown

North Beach is one of San Francisco's most complex neighborhoods, and the birthplace of its modern café culture. Originally a wet and dangerous encampment of shacks and sheds, it was once noted for the fact that unwary men were often knocked unconscious and conscripted as seamen on ships headed for China. This was the origin of the expression "to be Shanghai-ed."

North Beach has always had a decidedly Euro-bohemian flavor, but its identity is purely a San Francisco phenomenon. Hearty food, savory pastries, soothing wine, lively music, and instant camaraderie have long been hallmarks of this café-covered neighborhood.

Also referred to as the Barbary Coast, North Beach has been home to San Francisco's wild nightlife for decades, and hosts one of the city's few red-light districts, as well as what was once the first gay bar. Traditionally Italian-American in character, here family-oriented traditions coexist unhindered with San Francisco's laissez-faire attitude, creating an incubator for several very interesting developments. North Beach was the birthplace of the 1950's social and literary counterculture referred to as The Beat Generation. Not surprisingly its most prominent member, Jack Kerouac, once referred to the movement as "the Beat of the Street." Considering the amount of time they spent wandering North Beach's avenues and coffeehouses, it would be safe to assume he was referring to those of this district. In truth, the beat of North Beach has always been that of its café society.

Kerouac opened a million coffee bars
and sold a million pairs of Levis to both
sexes. Woodstock rises from his pages.

William Burroughs

I don't know, I don't care, and it
doesn't make any difference!

Jack Kerouac

It is an odd thing, but every one who disappears is said to be seen at San Francisco. It must be a delightful city, and possess all the attractions of the next world.

Oscar Wilde (Lord Henry, in *The Picture of Dorian Gray*)

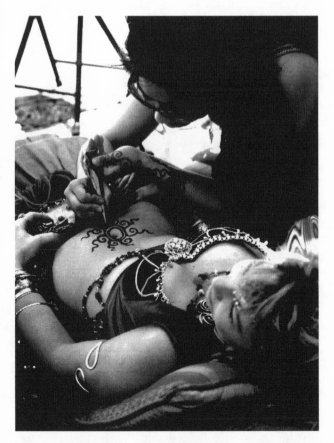

San Francisco is a mad city—inhabited for the most part by perfectly insane people whose women are of a remarkable beauty.

Rudyard Kipling

Caffe Trieste

601 Vallejo   San Francisco   415-392-6739

It's not much to look at, but with good reason Caffe Trieste is referred to as "Il Caffe di Tutti Caffe" (the Cafe of all cafes). Trieste was the first espresso cafe on the West Coast. It goes without saying that there were many famed San Francisco spots for dining, coffee, or carousing before Giovanni Giotta opened the Trieste in 1956. But it was only after he began serving traditional espresso and pastries in a live-and-let-live environment that the people of San Francisco saw that this was a place they really wanted to be. Trieste became ground zero for the impending cultural revolution known as the Beat Generation. Beat poets such as Ginsberg and Kerouac regularly came by to work, talk, debate and think. Francis Ford Coppola found inspiration as well and wrote parts of The Godfather here.

History and influence aside, Trieste is also known to have some of the best coffee and baklava in the city. Additionally, the Trieste's Saturday afternoon sing-along operas are legendary events filled with community zeitgeist. After almost half-a-century, Caffe Trieste remains the vibrant bohemian Il Caffe di Tutti Caffe.

The following is an excerpt from the autobiography of Giovanni Giotta, Founder of Caffe Trieste, a work in progress by Kristen Jensen

In 1956, a café opened in North Beach, the Italian enclave of San Francisco. This small, rather dim room, with high ceilings and a wall-sized mural of Italian fishermen, became what is know as the first true Italian coffeehouse on the West Coast. The proud new owner, Giovanni "Gianni" Giotta, dubbed his new establishment the Caffe Trieste, after his homeport of Trieste, Italy. In that city, known for its historic cafés and where both James Joyce and Italo Svevo found inspiration, Trieste was reputed to make the best coffee in Italy. The North Beach café was immediately popular within the neighborhood, serving as a morning meeting place for Italian professionals and laborers alike. Espresso was not a drink commonly known to the average North American, but Gianni had learned the true way to imbue the spirit of Italy into his cappuccino, macchiatos, and of course, traditional espressos.

In the midst of this resurgence of tradition, Gianni also found an emerging breed of clientele. In the Caffe Trieste, the Beats discovered a coffeehouse like the ones they craved. From their cramped studios and decrepit residential hotel rooms, they came every day, turning the Trieste into their own version of a living room. Ginsburg, Kerouac, Ferlinghetti, Hirschman, Cherkovsky, Norse, Kaufman, and Corso; all the legends of the Beat generation followed a path that often brought them together at Gianni's place. From the early morning espresso to the late night wine, the writers found an undemanding backdrop for their working lives.

These days when now looking at Trieste's unimpressive storefront, it is hard to imagine the colorful lives it has engendered.

There is nothing slick here, no recessed lighting, no ferns, no palms, no Internet, nor any sleek and stylish modern surfaces. The menu on the wall behind the counter is quite dated, showing faded yet reliable favorites. The dusk red cement floor and glossy burnt-orange walls border a room with tall ceilings and tables topped with bright mosaic tiles. A pot-bellied stove and a wood telephone booth are just where they have been since the fifties. The jukebox is still stocked with antique forty-fives, mostly of operatic arias and Italian folksongs . The near life-sized mural on the back wall, a classical theme of fishermen repairing nets while their women gossip on the beach, has seen a vast ebb and flow of even more colorful characters since it was painted in 1957.

But this unassuming corner does hum with a constant creative magic, as if a vortex exists below the building that sends creativity up through the vents and into the citizens of this community. The long day that stretches from dawn until nearly midnight sees a flow of people who come to sit and discuss ideas for hours, or scratch earnestly in notebooks, or tap on laptop boards. Several times a week a movie star or rock musician is spotted in a corner. Half the crowd wouldn't dream of bothering them while the other half simply don't know and don't care. In the afternoon, families and tourists wander in. Taking their white

china cups to a seat, they notice the dozens of photos covering the walls, and the fascinating game of "find the Trieste celebrity" begins. Pavarotti gazes from his place of honor, and Bill Cosby, and Francis Ford Coppola, who found the place so Italian that he wrote much of the screenplay for "The Godfather" sitting next to the old phone booth. In the gathering darkness, the artists descend once again from their studios to discuss the day spent slaving over manuscript and canvas.

The line at the counter is nearly constant. Within a few years of opening the café, it was suggested to Gianni that he produce his own house brand of coffee. A small roaster was installed in the window of the adjoining storefront, which became the coffee annex, and Gianni and his sons experimented diligently until they found just the right combination of temperature and time to produce a coffee they could proudly offer to the public. Today, the Caffe Trieste brand of coffee is sold all over America, carrying the reputation of the best. That consensus is demonstrated every day by the cabdrivers and fishermen, executives and students, writers and painters, who stop by for their daily shot. Jim and Paul, who have ground coffee for generations of customers, recall the custom blend of each as they walk in the door.

One of Gianni's early customers was an Italian who had begun to import flavored syrups for Italian sodas. Gianni offered these sodas at the café, and one day the idea came to him to put some of the flavored syrups into coffee. Yes, it was Gianni who invented flavored coffee, a staple in coffeehouses all over today.

At the age of eighty-one, Giovanni Giotta, known affectionately as Papa Gianni, often entertains music lovers with opera arias during the Saturday family concerts, a tradition for almost thirty years. Papa Gianni is joined by family and friends amidst rearranged tables, where the mix of opera, Italian folk songs, old standards, and country is a crowd-pleaser. Gianni's son, Fabio, concertmaster and accordion virtuoso, affectionately refers to the production as an "Italian Lawrence Welk Show", and indeed, there is a homey, genuine quality to the show that is rare today.

Papa Gianni's passion for life, music and good coffee has made the Caffe Trieste a cradle of love and romance. Young men find the concert the perfect place to surprise their girlfriends with a ring, and the audience becomes family when he gets down on one knee before his beloved. Last summer, in the middle of the concert, a bride and groom came in the front door of the café. They had just gotten married at the church across the street, and before going to their reception, had decided that their first dance of married life would be at the Trieste. When they entered the café in their finery, the music stopped, and all eyes turned to them. Their request was taken graciously by the band. The music began, and they danced on the small floor in front of the counter. The audience was captured up in the romance of this impromptu celebration, as the couple in their beautiful clothes twirled and spun, looking deeply into each other's eyes. At the end of the song, the couple said their thanks, and slipped out the door in search of their future. Over the decades, couples have met here and fallen in love in this place where everything seems possible.

Today, Gianni's daughter-in-law, Adrienne, capably oversees the daily behind-the-scenes business of the café and coffee annex. Ida, Papa Gianni's granddaughter, keeps watch at the counter, easily bantering with customers in English or Italian, although she too is ready to eighty-six anyone who gets above himself. Fortunately, she hasn't yet resorted to the broom.

The Caffe Trieste is not a world icon like the Golden Gate Bridge. It is small and unassuming from the street, with only a small green sign to point it out. Many people stumble on it by chance. They soon find out how lucky they are.

Tosca

242 Columbus Avenue   San Francisco   415-986-9651

Tosca isn't much to look at from the outside, and that's part of its celebrity appeal. Though there is a large sign above the cafe that you can see for half a mile, you could still literally walk by Tosca one hundred thousand times and never think about entering. Unless of course one of two things happened. First, you noticed that the large crowd of people inside seemed to be very cheerful, or second, someone told you to meet them here. Either way, once you have gone inside you are hooked. Owned by celebrity-confidante Jeannette Etheredge, the latter situation is what most often brings in her customers, including many of the more 'well-known' clientele. Some of the names that have been regulars over the years at Tosca include Francis Ford Coppola, Robin Williams, Sean Penn, Mayor Willie Brown, Gordon Getty, Mel Brooks, U2's Bono, and Nicholas Cage. They have made a habit of having late-night drinks at Tosca with actors or musicians in town for one reason or another.

Opened originally in 1919, Tosca has an old-time quality now only seen in movies, where people walk into a 1940's-style cafe and all the neighborhood characters are already there, including Joe the bartender, Frank the hard-drinking regular, and Bogart, Bacall, Sinatra, and Callas. Red leather booths line the walls, providing good views of the center of the room. Chandeliers provide light to a wall-length painting of the gondoliers of Venice, while the jukebox plays a selection from its stock of Opera hits. Martinis are poured on a fairly regular basis, but the house specialty is a cappuccino with cream, brandy, and Ghirardelli brand chocolate. True, during the 50 and 60's the Beats would come through here, but after Etheredge took over in 1979 the place recaptured its upscale appeal. Like other North Beach oldtimers, Tosca has its fair share of tales. For example, Willie Brown made his final decision to run for mayor of San Francisco in the Tosca's famous poolroom. Perhaps this fame-derived celebrity and influence is inevitable for a cafe name 'Tosca,' just as is often the case for operatically-themed spots that go by the title 'Scala. ' Class is after all an ephemeral value, the more you try to define it the farther away you get.

DON'T ENVY BEATNIKS...
BE ONE!
Thrill your wife,-stun your neighbors! Crash the pad parties.. unobserved!
You, too, can be suave and uninhibited by purchasing TRADER HENRI'S do-it-youself
BEATNIK KIT
FOR LADIES AND GENTLEMEN
Each kit complete with a copy of PADRIEC SUEMUS O'SULLIVAN'S epic poem "HOWYA GONNA KEEP 'EM DOWN ON THE PENINSULA AFTER THEY'VE SEEN NORTH BEACH?" and the original signature and greetings from ERIC NORD "big daddy of the beatniks
This breath-taking value for only $6.95
Hurry! Hurry! Step inside and place your order with the bartender now!

Vesuvio Cafe

255 Columbus Avenue   San Francisco   415-362-3370

The most famous Vesuvio story goes like this: In 1960 Jack Kerouac was supposed to meet author Henry Miller in Big Sur, California. Instead, a nervous Kerouac sat at the bar slamming drink after drink, intermittently calling Miller and reporting that he was delayed. That delay lasted all night and Kerouac never made it to Big Sur. The story is often retold because it is a good illustration of both Kerouac and of Vesuvio. Each represents a heady mixture of creativity, haphazardness, and pathos. Appropriately, Beat poet Alan Ginsberg previewed portions of his groundbreaking poem "Howl," at Vesuvio. "Howl" was eventually published by neighboring City Lights Bookstore, and was subsequently outlawed for its 'obscenity,' then liberated after a court battle led by City Lights founder and poet laureate Lawrence Ferlinghetti.

Opened in 1948 by Swiss-born Henri Lenoir, Vesuvio has always been a place for everyday people with an open-minded appreciation for the diversity of the human spirit and a taste for inexpensive liquor any time of the day or night. Customers like the Beats are just one example. If you talk to the bartenders or any of the regular clientele you will generally find the same esprit de coeur which has made it attractive to artists, poets, and wandering travelers for over half a century.

Vesuvio has history. The walls and stairways are covered with old photos and other keepsakes, many from the Beat era. On the outside of Vesuvio is a mural, one of many decorations, that reads, "When the shadow of the grasshopper falls across the trail of the field mouse on green and slimey grass as a red sun rises above the western horizon silhouetting a gaunt and tautly muscled Indian warrior perched with bow and arrow cocked and aimed straight at you it's time for another martini."

Stella Pasticceria e Caffé

446 Columbus Avenue   San Francisco
415-986-2914

Owned by the Santucci family, Stella's has been a North Beach fixture for well over half a century. Through all of these years the family remains very involved in the life and culture of the neighborhood. As a pasticceria, Stella's has a wide selection of delicious cookies, cannoli, cakes, and other goodies. It is also famous for having the most fabulous Sacripantina, which around the holidays need to be ordered well in advance.

Caffé Puccini

411 Columbus Avenue   San Francisco
415-989-7033

In a town with so many excellent coffee selections, no one is going to agree on who has the best cappuccino in San Francisco. But Puccini is definitely on the list. With very large picture windows, nice-sized tables, and comfortable seats, inside and out, Puccini is a perfect yet unpretentious spot for checking out the local scene. Ladies in particular seem to be very fond of Puccini's ambiance, especially the music selection, and find it a great meeting point for friends.

Mario's Bohemian Cigar Store

566 Columbus Avenue   San Francisco   415-362-0536

Mario's Bohemian Cigar Store. The name alone evokes a sense of texture and a timelessness found cozying up to a barstool. Mario's is a cafe that serves as a touchstone for many in North Beach. The low lighting, soft Miles Davis and intimate size wrap around you, asking only that you sit back and enjoy the mood. My favorite time of the day is just as the sun is sending long shadows through the window, across my cappuccino, or house made campari, and into the hand of cards I've just dealt. It is the kind of place where I can spend an hour and feel as if I've been somewhere.

Located strategically across the street from Mario's is North Beach's Washington Square Park, a main gathering place for music and art fairs, friends, families, and early morning Tai Chi practioners.

Many people like to go to Mario's specifically for its legendary meatball on focaccia sandwiches, apparently the memory of which have some making it their first stop upon arriving in San Francisco. One sandwich that will make you want to eat twice is the Grilled chicken marinated in garlic, white wine, olive oil and herbs, served with sliced onions, pepper jack cheese and Dijon mustard. Not quite a gourmet selection, but in the mouth it feels like it was made by Julia Child.

Caffé Roma

526 Columbus Avenue   San Francisco   415-296-7942

Opened in 1989, Roma has many attributes that you look for in a cafe. A good location on the sunny side of the street, ample seating, open windows, generous tiramisu, and a North Beach family at the helm are just a few. The Family Azzolini has been in the coffee business in San Francisco for almost three decades. The clan's father, Sergio, opened a coffeehouse here in 1977, and the children have been involved in aspects of the business ever since, eventually inaugurating the new Caffe Roma. Their clients are a fairly diverse and mellow bunch, including artists, restaurateurs, socialites, and neighborhood old-timers. A lot of people just drop in during a stroll down vibrant Columbus Avenue.

In addition to being a cafe, Roma is also a coffee roasting company. If you are looking for fresh roasted coffee, as in fresh from the roaster

20 feet away, and consider yourself a coffee-lover, then that is reason enough to come here. To display the seriousness of their dedication, the Azzolini's have placed portions of their roasting outfits inside of the cafes. At the Columbus Avenue location the fire-engine red roaster is located in the front of the cafe, where you pass it upon entering. At their second location on Bryant Street, across from the San Francisco Hall of Justice, the roasters are set in their own humongous alcove. Also on display are various cups and other memorabilia for purchase. Caffe Roma's high-quality blends are true to the coffee spirit, and are supplied to establishments and customers around the world, which is why this cafe is often featured in magazines such as Gourmet, Food & Wine, Conde Nast, and Coffee Journal.

Caffe Greco

423 Columbus Avenue   San Francisco   415-397-6261

A relative newcomer to North Beach in 1988, Greco has nonetheless gained a reputation of being extremely European and authentically 'old school North Beach.' Which says a lot for a cafe, even when it supplies a rack of the latest edition of international newspapers like Le Monde and the Herald Tribune. But the reasons for this praise are soon obvious. The huge picture windows frame seated patrons like a department store display, one which entices passersby to enter and join the collage. Most cafe lovers find this type of siren's call difficult to resist, with many eventually succumbing and going in to 'get something,' not quite sure what. Fortunately the Greco pastry and beverage selections are quite satisfying, like the tiramisu, fresh focaccia, prosciutto & mozzarella bagel, panforte, and Caffe Freddo Sambucca. Greco is also the main West Coast outpost for Illy's Coffee, an espresso purist's standard, or as the Illy family says, "the world choice for people who know and love coffee."

Opened and run by Hanna Suleiman, the Greco played a large role in the evolution of San Francisco cafe society in the early 1990's. According to Javawalk tour guide Elaine Sosa, Hanna and the Greco were instrumental in getting more permits issued by City Hall for curbside cafe seating. The ability for more cafes to offer curbside seating, versus patio seating or window seating, initiated a major resurgence of the Old World cafe society for which San Francisco was previously known.

People tend to fall in love with Caffe Greco, and discuss it passionately when mentioned. There is definitely a sexiness to the establishment and to its diverse clientele. Seating can at times be a challenge, especially if you are trying to get a table outdoors or at the window, but a recent expansion of the cafe into the adjacent store space has alleviated this situation.

The Steps of Rome

348 Columbus Avenue   San Francisco   415-397-0435

If you've ever done the Ibiza-Amalfi-Roma circuit, or dreamt of having done it, then the Steps of Rome will feel very familiar. This is the proclaimed capital of San Francisco "Euro-chic." Inside and out, Steps of Rome has the ambiance of a laid-back party on the Mediterranean coast. Regardless of age, you end up feeling young and gorgeous, partially due to the chatting of the friendly and very Italian staff, who also like to sing as well as flirt with the customers. It doesn't hurt that the food is delicious, the wine is good, the coffee is strong, and that the cafe is strategically located to get the maximum amount of sunshine possible in temperate San Francisco.

Among the many menu choices our favorites are the aromatic Penne Puttanesca, the seafood-filled Spaghetti ai Frutti di Mare, and any focaccia sandwich. Every selection goes nicely with either a cappuccino or a chianti, including the omelettes. Don't forget to have a piece of tiramisu.

Cafe Madeleine

300 California Street San Francisco   415-362-3332

Opened in 1999, Cafe Madeleine feels like San Francisco's version of "Breakfast at Tiffany's." The gorgeous metal & glass exterior encloses a sophisticated interior accented by high-ceilings, marbled countertops, long mirrors and fine woods.

The Cafe Madeleine food is as good as it looks. The French pastries are delicious, including tarts, croissants, palmiers, madeleines and florentines, as well as more international choices such as scones, muffins, brownies and cookies. The Cafe Madeleine gourmet sandwiches show that in San Francisco even a sandwich is worth the trip. Selections include Albacore tuna with capers, caramelized onions and jack cheese on an Italian Kaiser roll, Port Salut cheese and apple with candied walnut spread on a potato-rosemary roll, and our favorite, chicken breast with Balsamic onions, arugula and goat cheese. A second Cafe Madeleine is located on O'Farrell Street across from Macy's near Union Square, and is a smaller scale version of the original.

Delucchi

500 Columbus Avenue   San Francisco   415-393-4515

Caffe Delucchi has some pretty large footsteps to follow. Set on the corner of a major intersection on Columbus Avenue, surrounded by illustrious North Beach names such as Rose Pistola, Caffe Roma, Mara's, and Moose's, Delucchi needed to do something original. Fortunately it has, by delivering an eye-catching cafe with artistic design as its theme. Delucchi's tasteful exuberance for this topic can be seen inside and out. The exterior is a riot of stylish multi-colored tiles placed underneath the red latticework of a trellis awning. The building itself curves around the corner in a smooth, glass-accented "V." The smell of young jasmine vines wafts through the air as patrons sit in the modern cafe chairs to soak up the sun overhead. People-watching is at a premium here.

The triangular-shaped interior is modern and vibrant, highly detailed metalwork is in evidence at the bar. This attention to detail in even the smallest areas lends the cafe an atmosphere reminiscent of Barcelona. It's a rather unique look for San Francisco, but one that works at Delucchi.

Cafe Zoetrope

916 Kearny   San Francisco   415-291-1700

Cafe Zoetrope is an example of how to take an ordinary street corner and redefine it so that an entire intersection becomes your own. Located

at the cross-streets of Kearney and Columbus Avenue and formerly known as the Niebaum-Coppola cafe, Zoetrope is a landmark that can be seen for blocks. This effect is partially due to the Sentinel Building in which the cafe is situated, a triangular-shaped verdi-gris colored enigma with roots in the earlier part of the 20th century and style from Paris in the 19th. At the foot of the building are the cafe's striking black facade and brasserie-red awnings, the duo setting an attractive stage upon which patrons sit, relax and dine at delightful curbside tables.

Named for the production company of its founder, Oscar-winning director, writer and producer Francis Ford Coppola, best known for films such the Godfather trilogy and Apocalypse Now, the cafe is an extension of both the vineyard's harvest as well as Coppola's own love of the San Francisco cafe culture. The food is classic North Beach Italian, with an emphasis on the Bay Area's general desire for freshly prepared produce, cheese, olive oils, and pasta. Of course, the cafe also serves all vintages from the Coppola's various vineyards, including Zinfandels, Syrahs, Chardonnays and Merlots. Take heed, Francis has been known to enjoy the sun on nice days.

Jackson Place Cafe

633 Battery, One Jackson Place   San Francisco   415-225-4891

Wander past its various offices down narrow passages to the courtyard of One Jackson Place and you may find a surprise as big as Alice found inside the Looking Glass. The Jackson Place Cafe stands like a prop from Fritz Lang's METROPOLIS, and makes a statement that 'Design is Everywhere.' Clad in fitted sheets of burnished copper, this popular little cafe started life as a former flower stand. These days it sits under the green leaves of a nearby palm reflecting the rays of the overhead sun, much to the pleasure of local patrons.

North Beach

Buena Vista Cafe
2765 Hyde Street
San Francisco
94109
415-474-5044
The eclectic Buena Vista has some major history behind it, in that they were the first institution to bring authentic Irish Coffee to American shores back on November 10th, 1952. Evidently the drink was a huge success, and since then they've been lining up fans watching them line up and mix Irish after Irish.

Cafe Jacqueline
1454 Grant Avenue
San Francisco
94133
415-981-5565

Caffe Sapore
790 Lombard
San Francisco
94133
415-474-1222

Graffeo Coffee Roasting
735 Columbus Avenue
San Francisco
94133
415-986-2420
A major coffee supplier in the San Francisco area, Graffeo coffee is splendidly aromatic

Mara's Italian Pastry
503 Columbus
San Francisco
94133
415-397-9435

Michaelangelo Cafe
579 Columbus Avenue
San Francisco
94133
415-986-4058

Savoy Tivoli
1434 Grant Avenue
San Francisco
94133
415-362-7023
Good coffee, great people watching, and maybe some successful people meeting.

Spec's Twelve Adler Museum Cafe
12 Saroyan Place, 12 Adler Way
San Francisco
94133
415-421-4112

Victoria Pastry Co.
1362 Stockton St.
San Francisco
94133
415-781-2015
Established in 1914. The place for North Beach pastries, tiramisu, wedding cakes, as well as a good coffee. Located at the melding point between North Beach and Chinatown, you can meet many locals and old-timers just by hanging around the counter salivating. They'll waste no time in telling you how fantastic everything tastes. The square cherry puff pastry is not to be missed.

French Quarter

B-44
44 Belden Place
San Francisco
94104
415-986-6287
A Spanish-style tapas spot on the happening Belden, B-44 has everything a person suffering Barcelona-withdrawal could want: great design, tables indoors and out, attractive servers, and savory dishes. Good for day or night.

Caffe Bianco
39 Sutter Street
San Francisco
94104
Towering marble columns are just one reason that Caffe Bianco provokes passerby to look once, twice, then enter. Open for breakfast and lunch.

Grand Cafe / Petite Cafe
501 Geary Street
San Francisco
94102
415-292-0101
A large-scale Beaux Art-style restaurant and bar located at the Monaco Hotel in the Theater District. The statue by Albert Guibara is something to see, as are the art nouveau detailing. Some of the murals in the hotel lobby are immense.

Zuni Cafe
1658 Market St.
San Francisco
94102
415-552-2522
The Zuni Cafe has often been referred to as THE place to be in San Francisco, and there is no doubt that it is very popular and that the food is well-prepared. Fresh ingredients and a desire not to become stale and comfortable keeps the Zuni management on their toes, and regulars and out of towners feel that they are at a San Francisco hotspot even when just having a beverage.

The French Quarter

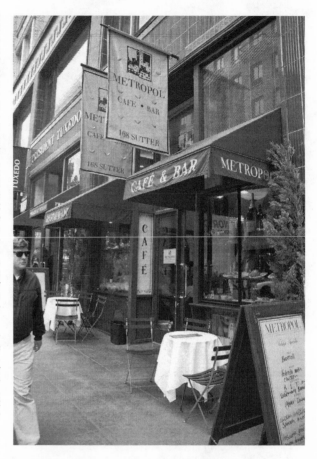

The influence of the French on San Francisco cafe culture is almost as great as that of the Italians. Though never a major immigrant group, there are now more than forty thousand French expatriates living in the region. Many are employed in areas such as technology and commerce, but several have established their own outposts of French colonization in a section of downtown San Francisco now called the French Quarter. This section, bordered by the streets Montgomery, Powell, Pine, and Post, is concentrated with French-influenced cafes, bistros, and brassieres. It is also home to the French Consulate, and one short mile away from the San Francisco Alliance Francaise. Together, this agglomeration constitutes a home-away-from-home for Francophones and Francophiles alike. At no time is this in greater evidence than during the annual July 14th Bastille Day festival, when the streets of San Francisco are awhirl with balls, dinners, dances, and parties.

In the eyes of some jaded purists these establishments might be quaint imitations of the originals. However, based not only on their popularity but also on their dedicated following of French citizens, it is more accurate to suggest that instead of imitations they are actually extensions of La Belle France.

San Francisco has its own concept of cafes, which might be a mix of different European concepts of cafes: English, Italian, Spanish, French...and as San Francisco looks like the only city in the U.S. to have that kind of cafe culture, it is unique.

Michel Richard
former Executive Director
Alliance Francaise
San Francisco

Café Bastille

22 Belden Place   San Francisco   415-986-5673

We all have cravings, and with many of us it's for a place to sit and feel like we woke up that morning in Paris. Some days it's for Edit Piaf's Paris, other days it's for Dimitri's. Cafe Bastille fortunately brings you both. Bastille's Bistro a la Paris Metro-styling is the anchor for the cafes on Belden Place, a former alley turned hip dining spot in the heart of San Francisco's Financial District. Night or day, Bastille and it's neighbors Tiramisu, Plouf, and B-44 seat non-stop crowds of regulars at their outdoor tables and indoor restaurants. The food at Bastille hits the spot, even if that spot happens to be vegetarian. Mushroom crepe served next to a fresh local mixed salad with walnut vinaigrette is a good starter. But as with many French meals, they get better with the addition of either fish, fowl, pork or meat. We prefer the steaks. Cafe Bastille uses the freshest lean cut of beef in their special Steak Tartare with Frites, and the affordable Hachis Parmentier is generous enough to leave any meat and potatoes fan delightfully sated.

At times the ambiance at Bastille changes. When this happens, you may unexpectedly find yourself not in San Francisco or Paris, but in Nice or Barcelona. Regardless, travel is good for the soul.

Café de la Presse

352 Grant Avenue   San Francisco   415-398-2680

Cafe de la Presse, at the corner of Bush and Grant opposite the gates to Chinatown, is the de facto center of the French Quarter. This isn't necessarily due to its centrality, but rather to its visibility and proximity. The cafe, a combination cafe/bistro/international newsstand, is situated adjacent to the extremely hip and visually striking Hotel Triton. Guests from the Triton, many themselves hip and striking, often sit at de la Presse's tables. The cafe is also on the same street as the French Consulate and the German-based Goethe Institute, their patronage lending it an element of Euro-chic. Completing the scene are the vast supplies of foreign magazines and papers, large sun-loving windows, and a quite good onion soup ("gratinee"). On French holidays such as Bastille Day the Cafe de la Presse has special menus and prices, making it a mandatory addition to your itinerary.

Cafe Claude

7 Claude Lane   San Francisco   415-392-3505

With its bon-vivant atmosphere and the return of legendarily charming bartender, Mel, Cafe Claude has the best looking French wait-staff in San Francisco...and the food's quite good too. For both of these reasons it draws a steady crowd of revelers and diners to its doors. Many of the interior furnishings were retrieved from retired cafes in France, which explains why the curving zinc bar combined with red booths plus the waiters and a few glasses of Cotes du Rhone can result in pleasant moments of geographical disorientation.

On the menu are your standard French cafe options like endive salad with figs, almonds, and Roquefort cheese, small plates such as roasted garlic and brie, and classic entrees including Confit de Canard (duck), Civet de Lapin (braised rabbit), and sautéed Halibut Niçoise.

In addition to the food and location, another reason why Cafe Claude is so popular is that it has mastered the art of 'la fete.' The cafe is lively even when the fete is simply a small jazz band, but it gets absolutely Gallic when the party is the annual bash honoring the late chain-smoking, drug-popping, poetry-writing, sex-crazed French national anthem singer Serge Gainsbourg. Cafe Claude and nearby cafes Bastille, de la Presse, and Le Central are also famous for shutting down San Francisco streets for the outrageously large and festive Bastille Day celebration, probably the largest and wildest in North America. These fetes are not the kind you remember from high school French class. These fetes are fueled by the presence of the French Consulate, several thousand French expats, their dates, some of their children, several thousand more Francophiles, and your basic San Franciscans looking to party. Vive la France!

South Beach
South Park
South of Market
(SoMA)

All mankind is divided
into three classes: those
that are immovable,
those that are movable,
and those that move.

Arabian Proverb

South Beach is the showpiece of the revital-ized San Francisco waterfront. Formerly the home of abandoned docks and warehouses, South Beach is now home to restaurants, cafes, palm trees, festivals, condominiums, and the water-skirting baseball bleachers of Pacific Bell Park.

Inland from South Beach is the South of Market area, also known as SOMA. Over a span of three decades, SOMA has gone from a center of manufacturing to being the city's biggest source of stylish new office space, lofts, and nightclubs. It is also the location of San Francisco gems such as the Museum of Modern Art, Yerba Buena Gardens, the Moscone Convention Center, China Basin, multiple galleries and theaters, and a legion of excellent cafes.

Caffe Museo

151 3rd St   San Francisco   415-357-4500

"In Xanadu did Kubla Khan..." The rest of that verse escapes me, but whenever I see the San Francisco Museum of Modern Art (SFMOMA), I imagine the great pyramids being rebuilt with a brand new design. In fact, I see them with the same design used by Swiss architect Mario Botta when he created this modernist 225,000-square-foot temple to the arts. The Permanent Collection includes the West Coast's most comprehensive collection of twentieth-century art, and consists of approximately 20,000 works of modern and contemporary painting, sculpture, photography, architectural drawings and models, and media art forms such as video and multimedia installation work. The Caffe Museo is an extension of the design inspiration and themes of the SFMOMA itself. Set at the front of the museum facing 3rd Street and the Yerba Buena Center, the cafe's windows run its entire length and provide excellent viewing space for people-watching. The interior furnishings complement the sleek modernity of Botta's vision, with light woods substituted for the museum facade's burnt-sienna, and tables and chairs of black leather and chrome mimicking the alternating bands of black and white stone on the roof's towering truncated cylinder. After a few hours of viewing the photography collection or participating in a forum about modern masters, followed by a stint in the Museum Bookstore, the Caffe Museo is a relaxing spot in which to refuel. It is also a convenient and chic place to meet friends or associates, and though not the least expensive in the city, the food is tasty and affordable.

ne- house red or house white *minimum $5.00*

Catering Services and Take-Out Available

South Beach Cafe

800 Embarcadero   San Francisco   415-974-1115

"They claim we have the best pizza in San Francisco," says owner Michele D'Amico. "It's addictive." High praise indeed, but fortunately well-earned. The South Beach Cafe does have some of the best pizza in San Francisco, though in our opinion it can easily be equaled by the cafe's own chicken with gorgonzola sauce, a dish we often travel well out of our way to sample. The pizza can also be matched by the incredible Italian desserts, several unavailable anywhere else in the Bay Area.

Located on the palm-tree lined streets of the South Beach neighborhood, facing the water and magnificent views of the Bay Bridge and Oakland, the South Beach Cafe feels like you are on vacation even when it's raining. This impression is aided by the decor, a festive, modern look accented by colorful mosaic tabletops of inlaid tile. The music of Italian pop star Eros Ramazatti jams in the background while European soccer plays on the overhead television. Cafe chairs wait outside, providing ample seating for soaking up the rays of the sun and the breeze from the Bay. Newcomers to the South Beach Cafe wonder how they could have ever missed it, and surprised they should be, as it is often the location for many local television shows.

Caffe Centro

102 South Park Avenue   San Francisco   415-882-1500

Caffe Centro has that quality which many cafes desire: presence. Since its opening in 1992, Caffe Centro's presence has been that of focal point for the South Park area. Originally created as an upscale residential development back in the 1800s, tiny South Park soon lost favor as more desirable locations in the north of San Francisco reached prominence. Also known as Multimedia Gulch, in the 1990's South Park was the epicenter of the new convergence of technology, video games, and film. Investment money flooded into the area, increasing the pace of urban renewal in this haven for creative geniuses. Caffe Centro's clientele is a mirror of the new neighborhood, where artists, computer geeks, photographers, shopkeepers, and executives dressed in trendy jeans and slogan-bearing t-shirts are virtually indistinguishable from each another. More often than not, however, on a nice day customers just order their food and sit across the street in the park, discussing the day's events while watching dogs play. According to Centro owner Max Applegarth, "There's a lot of life in this little cafe."

Caffe Centro prides itself on sourcing their products from local Bay Area vendors, and on using as many organic ingredients as possible. Tasty choices include the grilled breast of chicken with provolone cheese on focaccia, and the pear & brie salad.

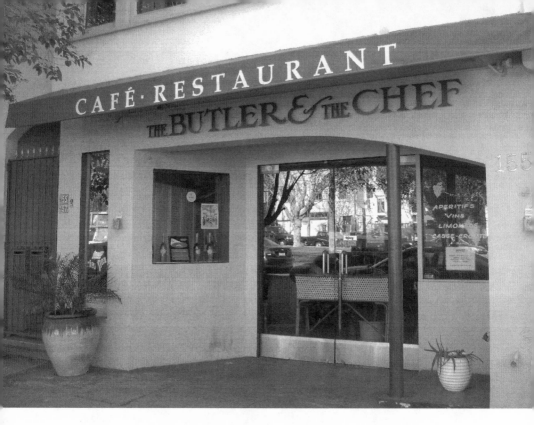

The Butler & The Chef

155-A South Park Avenue   San Francisco   415-896-2075

The Butler and the Chef is the newest addition to the circle of cafes around South Park. It was launched as an extension of an existing business specializing in antique bar and kitchen furniture from the early 18th-20th century France. The thinking behind its creation was that many of the pieces on display were for use in cafes, and in fact were from cafes. Why not therefore put them to use in an actual cafe? Fortunately, the partners moved forward with this concept, because the Butler & the Chef is a perfect petite cafe. Everywhere you look has a table that begs to be eaten on, or a chair that cries out for you to sit in. Vintage wine bottle holders, looking a bit like modern magazine racks, are suddenly the solution you have been searching for all of these years. Of course, none of this would be more than a life-sized display if the cafe itself weren't real, and the Butler and the Chef is definitely real. The food is good, the service is pleasant, the customers are interesting, and yes, the items are for sale.

A few words with Beat poet ruth weiss

What were your thoughts when you first came to San Francisco?

I first came to San Francisco in 1952. I hitch-hiked from Chicago, before the whole Beat-thing started. I thought then and now that San Francisco was more European than any other city in the United States, and I felt at home. I'm originally from Europe, we moved from Berlin to Vienna to get away from all the craziness at the time, and as you know Vienna has great cafe society. When I came to San Francisco I was in my bohemian period, but North Beach was in her bohemian period from way back. It's probably because the concept of cafes was very European, especially in old Italian neighborhoods like North Beach. Very bohemian.

So there was already a cafe society in San Francisco?

Think about it. Paris in the '20's and '30's like most places people lived in at the time was cold. You lived in a small, cold room and you didn't want to bring your friends back there. People went out to meet, they went to the warm and open cafes. That's a bit how San Francisco was. In San Francisco my place was small too, so where did I go to meet my friends?

What about the Beat scene around the cafes?

People came to San Francisco from all over the country, just like to the Hippie scene later, because it attracted a lot of artists, would be artists, those who liked to be with artists, and those who just liked art. People have a need to communicate. They need to communicate their thoughts. During the Beat scene most people didn't even know a lot about each others' backgrounds. But they still come out to exchange their personal thoughts and feelings. They did it in the cafes.
I remember places like Vesuvio's, it had folk singers and sawdust on the floor, and of course I remember the Co-Existence bagel shop. One night I was out at one of the spots, probably Vesuvio's, when I met this guy by the name of 'Specs.' He had moved here from the East Coast, and he said to me, "Man, where's the jazz in this town?" So I took him over to Fillmore. We walked from North Beach to "Bop City", where Miles and all the other jazz guys used to play. A couple of years later this guy opened the bar "Spec's," so he could have a place to hang out.

Any other thoughts?

You know, Hitler went after the cafes. Whenever a government is trying to destroy communication between people, they zero in on places like the cafes because they are key points of communication.

South Park Cafe

108 South Park Avenue   San Francisco   415-495-7275

Opened in 1986, the South Park Cafe was one of the first Bistro-style cafes in San Francisco. Its choice of courtyard-like South Park for its location was a stroke of genius. The art-oriented South Park neighborhood was just beginning its rise into a hip, hot San Francisco spot, and the surrounding South of Market district had barely begun its own renaissance. The South Park Cafe was a diamond in the rough, a true gem waiting to be discovered by the adventurous and open-minded. These days you don't have to be adventurous to go to the South Park Cafe, just looking for simple French dishes prepared in a modern yet classical Bistro style. Designed in natural colors and dark woods, the cafe exudes class as well as an almost family-like amicability. My favorite choice off the menu is their duck, when available, but that always tends to be my choice in a cafe that I know can do it justice. The steamed salmon is also quite good, as are the pastries and des-

serts. The wine selection is knowledgeable and what you would expect in an establishment that has made its mark on San Francisco for over fif-teen years. What is also memorable is that the service is open and friendly, and though it has few outdoor seats able to enjoy the views of the tree-lined oval park across the street, the cafe's large windows open to expose inside diners to the outdoors ambiance.

As with many San Francisco bistros, the atmo-sphere is inviting and the clientele is diverse and reflects the themes of the neighborhood. The South Park Cafe is a perfect place to go with friends when you want to sit a while, talk a lot, and eat food that will leave you satisfied.

Brainwash Cafe & Laundromat

1122 Folsom Street   San Francisco   415-861-food

As well-designed as the building is, as satisfying as the omelets are, as funky as the music can be, it is tempting to dismiss the Brainwash Cafe & Laundromat as a simple gimmick. True, way back in the early 1980's a laundromat in Champaign, Illinois started offering beer to its customers and made the local news. But it is a far cry from a few drinks to a

vibrant and active cafe, especially one set in San Francisco. This is not to say that the Brainwash has not had its own fair share of press. The owner, Jeffrey Zalles, has been covered in every media outlet from Smithsonian magazine to cable television's Food Network. The real reason for the interest, however, is that the Brainwash is a great place to visit.

Located in SoMA, the Brainwash gets sun through its multi-paned windows at least two-thirds of the day, a major premium in San Francisco. Add to that the fact that you can get a table almost anytime except during San Francisco's Weekend Brunch Rush Hours (10am-1pm, Saturday and Sunday anywhere in town). Plus in the evenings live entertainment often takes over, offering a range of options from spoken word to open mike comedy to musical performances. Combined, all of the above results in a cafe so engaging that it is much more convenient to bring an extra set of clothing with you than to go home. You can always wash the ones you're wearing at the laundromat.

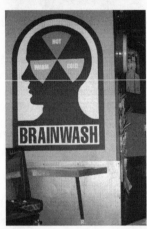

The Mission Noe Valley & The Castro

Cafe culture is public culture, a culture that resists the atomizing effect of coming home, turning on the television, and loosing touch with real people and real places. San Franciscans' passion for public engagement sustains our countless cafes, and the cafes return the favor.

Jaime Cortez
Galeria de la Raza

The Mission district, Noe Valley, and the Castro are three neighboring sections of San Francisco with strikingly different cultures. The Mission is primarily Hispanic in nature, and also plays host to two of the trendiest avenues in San Francisco, 16th Street and Valencia Street. The area is called the Mission district because like most major California cities, San Francisco was originally a mission settlement. In contrast, Noe Valley has the ambiance of a small ski resort town in the summer, with boutiques and shops lining its main thoroughfare, 24th Street. The Castro of course is famous for its central role as the capital of gay culture in the United States.

The Mission and parts of the Castro both play host to San Francisco's annual summer Carnaval parade (pictured left), an exuberant display of the harmony and diversity of San Francisco's people.

Samovar Tea Lounge

498 Sanchez Street San Francisco
415-626-4700

Samovar has the benefit of being in a perfect location for the person who really wants to chill out and reach a new level of bliss. The design - large windows, a light-filled room, exotic chairs and cushions, and a Zen-like decor including statues - prepares you for the true "tea lounge" experience. Tea is Royalty here, it invigorates instead of over-stimulates, and coffee is not served.

Samovar describes itself as "grounded in the values inherent to tea: relaxation, social intimacy, and health," as well as engaged in the 5,000 year old pan-culture/cross-continent tea experience, stocking over 100 premium small estate teas and herbal infusions from around world. The menu offers a creative variety of small plates ranging from edamame seasoned Korean nori, savory miso tahini noodles, ginger waffles with maple syrup, and green tea mousse in a Belgian chocolate cup, to sandwiches like zesty grilled tofu or Gouda & cured ham.

Atlas Cafe

3049 20th Street   San Francisco   415-648-1047

Opened in 1996, Bill Stone's Atlas Cafe is an oasis of serenity in this semi-residential Mission neighborhood. The exterior says '1950's gymnasium', while the interior is a comfortable 'coffeehouse in Havana.' Located near converted warehouses, avant garde theaters, publishing companies, multimedia firms, and San Francisco's main PBS outlet, the Atlas serves a diverse clientele. It also serves the tastiest roasted yam sandwich in Northern California, best eaten on the art-festooned outdoor patio. A magazine rack inside offers thoughtful and informative reading material for those interested in world events. Community-oriented, family-friendly and hip, Atlas stages live music performances, including Bluegrass, Jazz, and the Blues.

Cafe Flore

2298 Market Street   San Francisco   415-621-8579

Cafe Flore is a major meeting spot for the gay community, and is one of the first places to visit after an extended trip away from the city. This cafe has more than a few things going for it. First, it is located at a major intersection with great visibility. Second, it is in a neighborhood that gets more than its fair share of sun in fog-beleaguered San Francisco. Third, it has both a walled outdoor patio as well as an interior illuminated by floor-to-ceiling windows. Fourth, it is in the Castro district, a very animated locale where residents enjoy immensely both their socializing and their freedom. The building itself is a bit low-tech, but that works for a location formerly dedicated to automotive repair. The roof is made of corrugated sheet metal, and the support beams are made of fitted pipes. The overall effect is that of a greenhouse indoors, and with all of the plants and gossiping, that of a hothouse outdoors.

Le Zinc

4063 24th Street   San Francisco   415-647-9400

Le Zinc takes its name from a French expression for cafes. "Le zinc" is the pewter bar counter for which many of these establishments are fondly remembered. The creators of Noe Valley's 'zinc' have successfully designed a cafe/bistro that provides patrons with a tasty selection of breakfast, lunch, and dinner. Le Zinc has a very attractive and inviting exterior, and the interior is equally beguiling. It looks like a place where you can eat a long, slow, savory meal followed by a soothing tea or relaxing espresso. Attention to details is the key to this success. The dark plum facade is a tasteful contrast against the celadon building in which the length of Le Zinc is located. Inside, a combination of light colors, dark woods and clever lighting create a warm, convivial environment. The gated wine storage room, located behind the zinc-topped bar, is home to a carefully selected array of varietals and vintages.

Ritual Coffee Roasters

1026 Valencia   San Francisco   415-641-1024

Ritual is one of the emerging 'green cafes,' which make it a point to source their beans from providers practicing sustainable agriculture, as well as work to reduce the coffeehouse's impact on the environment. That being said, the coffee at Ritual has addicted devotees who swear it's the best this side of Seattle. They claim they can't make it through the day without a cup of this liquid gold.

Regardless of whether these claims are 100% true of not, what is true is that Ritual is one of the most popular cafes in the Mission District. The crowd is diverse but tends to be cool and hip and not too bad on the eyes. Because this is a San Francisco cafe, however, you're not bombarded with the "we're so cool and hip" attitude. Art exhibitions are regularly updated on the cafe walls, and the great natural lighting helps enhance the colors of not only the work, but also of the bright red that is part of Ritual's logo and theme.

Seating could be considered ample, if the place wasn't so often full of fans. In the back is a large coffee contraption, which Ritual uses to fill its many orders for coffee to go, as well as to the number of retail outlets around the Bay Area that carry its delicious beans.

Dolores Park Cafe

501 Dolores   San Francisco   415-621-2936

Dolores Park Cafe has the good fortune of large windows, a sunny exposure, good fare, cool patrons, and a view of one of San Francisco's biggest spectacles/meeting spots, Dolores Park.

Dolores Park is where people go to lie in the sun and catch some rays, have a picnic, watch a play, listen to a band, play tennis, frolic with dogs, protest social injustice, or celebrate practically anything. It's a very "San Francisco" place, and the Dolores Park Cafe has a great view of it all.

Added benefits include an outdoor patio, great pastries, and a lunch counter if it gets too busy to find a chair. Considering the block now also hosts foodie favorites such as the Bi-Rite gourmet grocery market, the world famous Tartine bakery, and the hard to get a reservation for Delfina restaurant, to name a few, the Dolores Park Cafe seems to be at the right place at the right time.

Maxfields House of Caffeine

398 Dolores   San Francisco   415-255-6859

Only a block away from popular Dolores Park, Maxfields sits on the corner of Dolores and 16th Street, giving it an unvarnished view of trees, churches, and the mellower aspects of one of the city's most vibrant neighborhoods. For that reason its own mellow vibe makes it a desirable place to go meet a friend, have some coffee, read a book, or work on your computer.

Artwork lines the walls, and there are comfortable couches from which you can admire it.

In some ways Maxfields is so low key that you might not even notice it, especially when driving by in a car. But when you're in the mood for what it offers, it can be love at first sight.

Maxfields has the noticeable high ceilings and windows of many San Francisco cafes

Revolution Cafe

3248 22nd Street   San Francisco   415-642-0474

Formerly called Papa Toby's Revolution Cafe, an extension of the popular Momi Toby's Revolution Cafe & Art Bar in Hayes Valley, the official name now is just "Revolution Cafe" (as in Che, the revolutionary). However the most revolutionary aspect of the cafe is not its funky tropical theme, or incredible amount of open air access, but the fact that people who discover it for the first time have an interior mental revolt about not having heard of it before.

The spot is cool, with great people watching, outdoor seating, laid back atmosphere, a very eclectic clientele, and often music events at night.

The Revolution Cafe is so popular among those in the know that apparently they're not talking about it to their friends, because you can just sit in a chair and watch people walk by for the first time with a startled look on their faces, undergoing a mental revolution about their new discovery.

The cafe serves wine, beer, coffee and tea, which all go well with the ambiance. It doesn't hurt that it lies in one of the warmest neighborhoods in San Francisco.

Coconut
$

Mexican Wedding
Cookies
with walnuts
$ .75

Shortbread
$ 1.25

Valrhona chocolate bite topped
with ganache
$2.00

Chocolate Hazelnut
Tart
Scharffen Berger chocolate
with toasted hazelnuts
$6.00 ~ small
$ ~ large

Tartine

600 Guerrero   San Francisco   415-487-2600

As popular as Tartine is, and it is very, very popular for its French-influenced baked creations, fresh coffee, fine wine and trendy location, many patrons don't know that it began in Mill Valley (Marin) and then moved to San Francisco. This is interesting because one morning several years ago I went to the Mill Valley shop only to find an empty store, so recently vacated that there were still puddles of water on the floor. Befuddled and disappointed Mill Valley residents stood outside the windows looking in, shocked by their unexpected loss.

Well, their loss became San Francisco's great gain. Tartine is one of the city's culinary gems, and has earned mentions in magazines and newspapers and on radio and television across the globe. It also has a first class cookbook published, named of course "Tartine."

As with most cafes in the area, the ceilings are high, the windows are large, and if possible, there are seats both inside and out. The food isn't inexpensive, but it is unforgettable.

Above: The Blue Bottle Coffee Company's very small but very busy shop window, located in Hayes Valley

The Haight
Hayes Valley
Western Addition
& The Panhandle

Folks visit cafes to relax, reflect, read a book, sometimes to socialize. As Howard Schulz says, they are an extension of one's living room. Cafes are great for lounging -- for "coffee house lizards", as I like to say. As a bohemian enclave, it's only natural that San Francisco would have a well-established coffee house scene. Plus, people have been slacking in these parts since the 1800s -- it's a big part of who we are, we really appreciate our down time. While places like Seattle try to emulate San Francisco as coffee towns, they still are the new kids on the block. San Franciscans have been doing this gig a lot longer, and have got it down pat.

Elaine Sosa (aka Javagirl)

Before the 1989 Loma Prieta earthquake, Hayes Valley was barely a blip on the map. The community was hardly ever noticed, and for decades sat in the shadow of a towering freeway overpass. However, when the road's infrastructure was severely damaged by the quake and the city subsequently decided to tear it down, Hayes Valley saw the light of day for the first time in years. This light continues to shine on the community, and has filled it with cutting-edge clothing & shoe stores, furniture shops, fine art video rentals, and cafes. It is indeed now known as one of the coolest spots in town.

Up the road from Hayes Valley sits the beginning of Haight Street, which runs all the way to the edge of Golden Gate Park. In the part closest to Hayes Valley, known as the "Lower Haight," the street has its own culture of urban grooviness. Farther down the road begins the "Upper" Haight, otherwise known as Haight-Ashbury, the home of Flower Power, the Summer of Love, and the Grateful Dead.

Absinthe

398 Hayes Street   San Francisco   415-551-1590

Owned by Billy Russell-Shapiro and set in the romantic style of the 19th century, Absinthe is a place that you find reasons to visit often. One reason is the friendly, gracious welcome you receive upon entering this Hayes Valley locale, whether you chose a cafe table in the front, an elevated seat at the 30-foot long cherrywood bar, or a booth in the full-service restaurant specializing in Southern France-inspired fare.

The bar is a regular destination for many, offering a substantial selection of wines, spirits, and Pastis. It is also where you will find several patrons in the process of consuming Absinthe's signature drink, the Ginger Rogers, a sublime combination of a Mojito with a Mint Julep and spicy ginger syrup. There is nothing more pleasurable on a Friday evening than sitting at the bar to a dozen oysters with a glass of Pinot Noir and a side order of the award-winning Frites with aioli sauce or slices of Grilled Portobello in balsamic. The food is fresh, de rigueur in San Francisco, and delicious. The Cassoulet l'Absinthe has been said by customers from France to be as authentic as dishes they ate as children. The Coq au vin with free-range chicken is equally original. Even simple side dishes such as Spinach with Garlic are to be relished. Do not leave without sampling dessert, including the near-erotic Lavender Creme Brulée.

Designed by architects Strauss Associates and Kathleen Rose Disston Interior Design, Absinthe sets the stage for the esprit de la Belle Époque. Period specific tin panels line the ceiling, muted burgundy-red walls are adorned with vintage Absinthe posters or photographs of modern Paris, and flowing multi-colored drapes, soft lights, well-placed mirrors, and the changing but perfect music selection all conspire to put you in a mood for casual elegance and fun.

Frjtz

581 Hayes   San Francisco   415-864-7654

Frjtz is a funky design-oriented cafe with locations in Hayes Valley and Valenica Street, and
is a newer spin on the San Francisco phenomena
of California-style 'crepe and coffee' houses.
Instead of serving California-style crepes with
names like the Santa Fe or the Monte Carlo,
Frjtz offers Belgian crepes and fries ("frites").
The pairing is heavenly. My past favorites have
been a combination of the Lichtenstein (fresh
strawberries with sour cream and wild berry
coulis) and the Van Gough (Lemon, butter and
sugar). Whenever customers saw my concoc-
tion they asked which it was off of the menu,
then proceeded to the counter to order it.

But don't forget that Frjtz has frites, and
these are quite large on the menu as well.
One of the cool things about them is that
they can be combined with various types of
ketchup, mustard, and other dipping sauces. If
this sounds plebeian to you, just try the ginger
orange mayo, the creamy wasabi mayo, or the
fantastic ponzu ketchup.

Hayes, Haight, & Divisadero

ets Clockwise from top left (opposite page): Cafe Abir, Cafe Abir, Blue Bottle Coffee, Bean Bag Coffee House, Momi Toby's Revolution Cafe, Momi Toby's, Cafe Abir

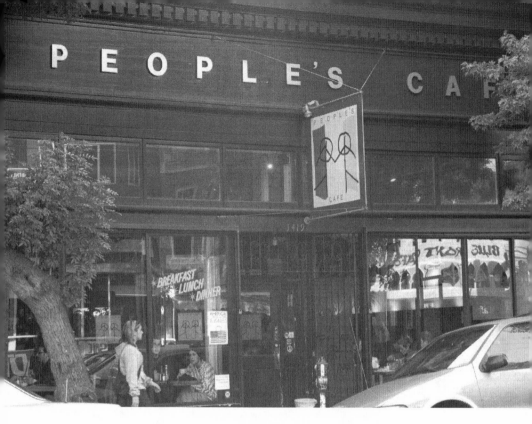

People's Cafe

1419 Haight Street   San Francisco   415-553-8842

A verbal allusion to the 1960's-era Berkeley epicenter of social revolution, the People's Park, the People's Cafe is an experience rich in symbolism. Set at the vibrant gateway of the Haight-Ashbury neighborhood, the People's Cafe is literally a window onto this world. One can sit here for hours quietly sipping a hot cider or herbal tea, contemplating the styles, fashions, and virtues of the eclectic populace of the Haight. One can munch on a vegetarian sandwich or a buttery Madeleine while gazing at the comings and goings of those who live, work, and hang out on this street. One can savor the aroma of the many blends of coffee while arriving at a nerve-tingling solution for world peace. In sum, one can chill out at the People's Cafe.

High ceilings, large windows, white walls, and vertical accent lighting encourage a feeling of spaciousness. Interesting and innovative local artists are often on display. Though in business for several years, the cafe is so well kept that newcomers often have the impression that it only recently opened. The friendly staff of hard-working veterans behind the counter, however, would disagree with this assessment. In this youth-influenced culture, it is ironic that more credibility is gained from the cafe's relative vintage than from its modernity.

In the end, the People's Cafe is indeed the people's cafe. Pleasant, open, and good for a home cooked breakfast as well as a day long lunch, it has some of the best seats in San Francisco for sitting, meeting, and absorbing the beautiful and complex layers of the citizenry.

One World Cafe

1799 McAllister Street   San Francisco   415-776-9358

The colorfully detailed stained-glass windows and the charming San Francisco-school of architecture exterior are just two reasons for visiting the One World Cafe. Offering everything from tuna & turkey to falafels & chai mochas, the One World has successfully established an outpost of cafe society in the Golden Gate Park neighborhood known as the Panhandle. In addition to great natural lighting, gourmet coffee, and healthy sandwiches, One World is also a mecca of the San Francisco comedy scene. In San Francisco the cafes have become prominent venues for the comedy circuit, and One World is a well-known promoter of this much needed art form.

Mojo Bicycle Cafe

639 Divisadero   San Francisco   415-440-2338

Mojo Bicycle Cafe is based on one of those San Francisco formulas that can't miss. Find a slightly below-ground location on a busy street in a neighborhood where a lot of interesting people live and don't want to leave. Put it in a fixed up Victorian building. Add a lot of warm, honey colored wood and natural light from windows. Be dog friendly. Put a garden patio in the back, hidden from view so it's almost like a little oasis where you can drink coffee, beer, or wine. Make sure the beer includes Red Stripe, and the wine is good enough for people who live 40 minutes from Napa. Offer a breakfast, brunch and dinner menu so people can eat well and at a reasonable price.

Then say, "Aha, we're right near one of the biggest bike paths in the City - Golden Gate Park and the Panhandle," and add your well-supplied and super-friendly bike shop to the mix - because frankly that's the kind of store you wanted to open anyway - and now you have one of the great cafe success stories of our time.

Really, this place is never empty, and when you come, you don't ever feel like leaving. "Mojo" is right, this place has it, even if you don't have a bike.

A cafe, at its best, offers a refuge from the world. It can provide a relaxing and comfortable environment to read, converse with friends and, of course, sip some energy raising coffee, tea or hot chocolate.

Dan Storper,
Founder of Putumayo World Music

Profile: Putumayo World Music

According to Dan Storper, Co-Founder of Putumayo: "How did the 'Music from the Coffeelands' CD come about? For quite a while we had been providing many cafes with CDs to play and sell in their cafes. In 1997, several cafe owners asked us to create a CD which featured music from coffee-growing countries. That led us to create 'Music from the Coffeelands.' The success of that CD led us to create a follow-up, 'Music From the Coffeelands II (The Refill)'. Music is a critical component in the cafe experience and for those CDs, I sought music which helped create a comfortable, soothing yet gently uplifting environment." One of the songs from the second disk is by a young Ethiopian singer by the name of Ejigayehu Shibabaw , known by her stage name, Gigi.

"Ethiopia is the birthplace of coffee, thanks to the goatherd Kaldi who over one thousand years ago noticed his goats getting peppy after nibbling on wild coffee beans. Fortunately for all of us, coffee didn't remain goat food for long. Coffee is still important in Ethiopia as it remains one of the most important exports as well as an essential part of the Ethiopian diet and community life.

Fifth child in a family of ten, Ejigayehu 'Gigi' Shibabaw was raised in an isolated village by socially conscious parents who'd turned their backs on the squalor of the city. Her family's life was directly dependent on the water from the river Ardi that was used to irrigate their coffee plants. A loyal daughter with a rebellious streak, Gigi sought her artistic fortunes abroad when her tradition-minded father initially forbade her to make her way in the world as an entertainer. Seeing the world stage as her true home, Gigi relocated to San Francisco at age 24.

Gigi describes 'Guramayle' as a love song to a child of the Diaspora. Guramayle are black tattoo spots on the upper gum above each tooth that some tribes in northern Ethiopia apply to adorn their smiles. It is also a word used to describe a pretentious person who mixes foreign words into their native language to appear superior. Gigi reclaims this derisive term as a positive notion reflecting the multitude of influences on Ethiopians living abroad. 'Let him speak in French, in English if he wants / Sing in Italian, let him swear in German / Honey flows from his mouth, sweet elocution / Let Him speak, let him exult / How he brightens my day / I miss your rap, my handsome city boy."

San Francisco has the best cafe culture that that I've personally experienced out-side of Europe. In fact, I have often found that the only one I can really compare it to is the cafe culture in Paris, which I often do. You can simply stroll down so many of San Francisco's sidewalks and find cafes, unknown and unadvertised, where you are able to drop in have a very nice time.

Spencer Christian, ABC Television Personality and Wine Connoisseur

I think that our cafes give San Francisco a special flavor. When I hear the word "cafe" I usually think of North Beach and the Beatnik era. I realize, however, that the word has become somewhat more mainstream and inclusive, and today a cafe can be anything from an outdoor coffee shop to tables in a bookstore to a small intimate restaurant or even a nightclub. Still, the 'cafe' idea is very European and everyone says San Francisco is very much like a European city.

Merla Zellerbach, The Nob Hill Gazette

It has often been said that San Francisco is reminiscent of the great European cities. The cafe life here also gives many San Francisco neighborhoods the feel of an artist colony - where philosophy is discussed, art is inspired and music is played.

Dean Deborah Berman, San Francisco Conservatory of Music

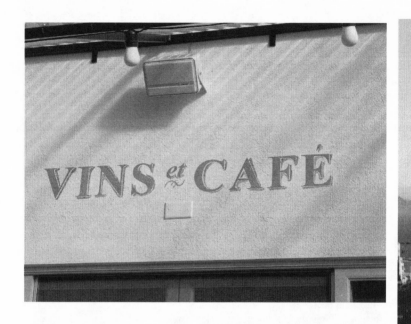

Russian Hill Polk Street & Nob Hill

Cafes are places where you can find inspiration and work things out - there is a certain element of boredom in a cafe, which leads to a strong need to do something while remaining seated at a table, and your choices are somewhat limited in that position. Reading, writing, composing poetry, musing in general, are activities which fit the situation. If compatible friends or acquaintances are present, once again the limits of the situation will lead to the sharing of thoughts rather than to more athletic pursuits. Being away from home also helps artists and writers to avoid the mundane - it's a homey atmosphere without the feeling that you should be doing the laundry or washing the dishes.

San Francisco has a wonderful European flavor, partly because it's a walking town, and partly because it has such great cafes - North Beach on a Sunday afternoon is like an Italian city, and you get a sudden feeling that many driven Americans could have a hidden streak of laziness - a guilty pleasure that also has something to do with the attractions of the cafe.

Elizabeth Stroud, Museum of Craft & Folk Art

Russian and Nob hills have long dominated the upper strata of San Francisco real estate and society. Located on steep precipices with varying views of the bay, Alcatraz, the southern peninsula, Oakland, and downtown San Francisco, both of these neighborhoods are often equated in the minds of many with success and sophistication. Polk Street is a major thoroughfare for these neighborhoods, as are California Street and Hyde Street. All three are studded with charming boutiques, cafes, restaurants, and access to various cable car routes.

La Boulangerie de Polk

2310 Polk   San Francisco   415-345-1107

Owned by French-born Pascal Rigo, who has built a 'petit empire' of bakeries and restaurants in San Francisco since the late '90's. Rigo has definitely found his way into the heart of many San Franciscans. There are scores of fabulous bread and pastry bakers in the region, but only he has yet to make 100% authentic chaussons aux pommes (apple turnovers) good enough to bring back fond memories of your last trip to France. Add to this his irresistible Macaroons de Paris, traditional and hard to find pains d'epice (Burgundy spice bread), red fruit tartes, sliced sausage and cornichon baguettes, and large or small palmiers, and you're going to start wondering if the word 'diet' ever existed. Rigo goes for an authentic, but not obsequious, French ambiance and design in his stores, which vary depending on regional theme. In addition, the staff is always nice and friendly, a true reflection of how the French actually behave in boulangeries. Pass the Madeleines.

Sugar Cafe

679 Sutter   San Francisco   415-441-5678

The Sugar Cafe looks like an uber-chic lounge for the uber-hip, uber-good looking, and uber-rich. Fortunately for cafe lovers, looks can be pleasantly deceiving.

There is no doubt that chic design was top of mind, but along with great style came a great atmosphere. The Sugar Cafe is warm and welcoming, and there is no dress code or minimum limit to enjoy it. The fireplace is a popular place to sit because it's eye-catching and near the large windows that allow natural light into the front section. The back section of the cafe has ultra-high ceilings and modern lighting. The coffee and cafe fare are reasonably priced for the neighborhood, and the cocktails and mixed drinks are extremely popular at night, when the Sugar Cafe starts feeling a bit more like the Sugar Nightclub... and that's uber-sweet.

Caffeine addiction is possibly the dirty little secret of cafes, but above and beyond that, cafes are a place to connect with other people. Not only visually, but with conversation and drinking together as well. It's very social.

David Latimer, Publisher, Cups a Cafe Journal

Profile: CUPS, A Cafe Journal

According to Publisher David Latimer, "CUPS was certainly reflective of a national movement that increased consumers sophistication about coffee and chronicled the growth and development of the cafe space as a "third place" to gather and socialize and perform (poetry readings etc.) which was not a bar or the home. The magazine produced 100 issues in 10 years. I bought CUPS from its original publisher, and after CUPS stabilized I began to grow the distribution first to Portland and Seattle, then Chicago, and finally I bought another magazine called Java Journal in NYC and took it national. We changed it to a monthly and had full color and glossy paper. We launched a trade magazine called Coffee Works and a series of Coffee coupon books for Boston , Seattle, Chicago and New York, We began CD compilations of spoken word poets and then a record label called "In Cafe". We also sponsored a major fund raiser for AIDS at the Palace of Fine Arts with most of the great poets and had fun doing other stuff. I finally sold the magazine to Christian Ettinger in 1998."

CUPS published its final issue a year after the sale. By that time, cafe culture had been completely embraced by America on a national level, partially due to the innovative efforts of magazines like CUPS.

The Cups Anthology 1994
Real Writing by Real People

i'm a Peet's Coffee man.
my favorite is the Peet's on polk between vallejo
and broadway.
don't get me wrong,
i know Starbucks is the evil empire
but when you're in an airport in akron and you
see one of those green kiosks
it's "aaaaaaaaaaaaah" in slow motion,
rainbows,
wheat growing,
very spielberg.
the problem is i drink black coffee and am
always forced to stand in line behind thirty
yuppies ordering their
fourteen-ingredient signature drink:
"yes, give me a double-decaf no-foam
butterfly-friendly soy-milk latte
with a twist of meyer's lemon and a shade-
grown caramel-rinse and make it
trapezoidal"
people, coffee is not a toy, its a tool!
it's hot bitter dirty water with a buzz.
there should be two lines,
one for normal people
one for fuffy twees

- will durst, comedian and social commentator

The Marina, Pacific Heights & Presidio

The Marina district began as cow fields and wetlands, and is now one of the most fashionable neighborhoods in the city. After the Great Earthquake of 1906, the rubble of San Francisco was transported to the Marina for use as landfill. This landfill was expanded and refined when the area was selected as the location for the 1915 Panama-Pacific International Exposition. Today's Marina district stretches between four major recreational and cultural parks: Fort Mason, the Presidio, Crissy Field, and the Marina Green.

Up the hill from the Marina are the aeries of Pacific Heights. Long in competition for status against other more established neighborhoods such as Nob Hill and Russian Hill, Pacific Heights enjoys some of San Francisco's most stunning views and beautiful homes.

On the other side of this hill sits the legendary Fillmore district, a major entertainment and shopping venue since 1906. Jazz, Rock and Roll, and Blues musicians, as well as poets such as Kerouac and Ginsberg, found a haven for their art in the Fillmore. From the 1920's through the 1960's the Fillmore was also home to San Francisco's largest African-American and Japanese-American communities, though both have been greatly affected by the politics of the time. Fortunately, though the modern Fillmore has lost some of its musical and cultural past, it is more than ever a home to cafes.

Fillmore Street

Clockwise from top left (opposite page): Curbside Cafe, La Mediterranee, Bittersweet Chocolate Cafe, Vivande, Elite Cafe, Florio, The Coffee Bean & Tea Leaf, The Coffee Bean & Tea Leaf

PlumpJack Cafe

3127 Fillmore   San Francisco   415-563-4755

Some cafés are made for special occasions. They don't have to be big occasions, they just have to be special, like birthdays, anniversaries, promotions, engagements, parents in from out of town, best friends from college visiting, or the fact that today is Friday. PlumpJack is that kind of cafe. Upscale enough for the big life events, cool and casual enough for even the flimsiest excuse to have a delicious dinner. Located on trendy Fillmore Street in the bustling Cow Hollow section of the Marina district, PlumpJack successfully creates an environment of relaxed elegance. Named after the Shakespeare character, Sir John Falstaff, the cafe is a sister property to the nearby PlumpJack Wine Shop, Balboa Cafe, MatrixFillmore club/lounge and PlumpJack Inn (Squaw Valley, Lake Tahoe). Like each of these, a premium is given to design, service, and selection. The design comes from the team of Leavitt/Weaver, who have melded complementary layers of soft colors, wall panels, and metal architectural accents and lighting into what is now known as the PlumpJack style. The food of course lives up to the setting, and is widely praised by food critics. We recommend absolutely anything with risotto, fish, or poultry.

The Grove Fillmore

2016 Fillmore Street   San Francisco   415-474-1419

The Grove Fillmore in Pacific Heights is, as one regular describes, "Really cool and perfect for this neighborhood." How could it not be? Keeping similar concepts found at the original Grove on Chestnut Street, the Grove Fillmore combines good food, wine, coffee and tea with some of the best people-watching (and people-meeting) a cafe could desire. It is a neighborhood destination, whether you're destined to quietly read a good book, discuss the state of the world, or compare last night's adventures.

Japantown

"San Francisco is fortunate in having quite a large proportion of the educated, cultured and prosperous Japanese. The Nippon Club at 740 Taylor street, composed of Japanese business and professional men, is unquestionably the best appointed and most prosperous foreign club in the city. It occupies a three-story brick building, designed and built for its purposes."

San Francisco Examiner. 23 December 1923

Before World War II and the forced internment of the Japanese-American population by the United States government, Japantown was a prosperous community in San Francisco. The area near Fillmore and Post, known as "Little Tokio" or Nihonmachi, teemed with shops and shrines and other meeting places for these first and second generation immigrants. Following the Federal government's lead, in 1942 local leaders declared the district a "slum area," creating a de facto forced evacuation. Left with few remaining material possessions and over three years of austere life in the camps, the Japanese-American internees were eventually released after the War to put their disrupted lives back together.

Two decades later a new Nihonmachi was built, with the 1968 opening of the three-block long Japantown Center. The Center itself is a monument to the indomitable will of this neighborhood. The Japantown Center today houses a variety of enterprises, including Japanese baths, bookstores, record stores, kimono shops, a video and anime outlet, a multi-screen movie theater, and of course, restaurants. Each street has its own building: Kinokuniya Building on the first block, Kintetsu Mall on the second, and the Miyako Mall, home to the Radisson Miyako Hotel, on the third. Connected by an open plaza and an overhead bridge, the three buildings offer a very pleasurable opportunity to take in the daily life of this unique community. You can also walk outside to the pedestrian-only Buchanan Mall, completed in 1976. The cobbled street of this area and the twin stone fountains, combined with the traditional Japanese architecture and a view of the Centers' towering Peace Plaza, come together to display both old and new aspects of the modern Japantown.

The Center also plays host to the San Francisco Taiko Dojo, the nation's premier school for the art of Japanese ceremonial drumming, or Taiko. The Taiko Dojo has received numerous international awards, and San Francisco has actually declared an official Taiko Dojo Day. Taiko is a beautiful form of music, one that gets the blood racing and the pulse pounding, as the beat of the drums are not only heard but felt in your entire body. Fortunately you are guaranteed to be able to see them play at least twice a year, once in April during the annual San Francisco Cherry Blossom Festival, and once in the Fall at a joint concert in Berkeley. Both of these opportunities not only allow you to see the San Francisco Taiko Dojo, but also Taiko groups from Sacramento, Los Angeles, Hawaii, and different cities in Japan.

In a spirit of mutual history, Japantown organizations are also supportive of various Pacific-American celebrations as well, including the annual Aloha Festival in the Presidio.

May's Coffee Shop

1737 Post Street/Japantown Center   San Francisco   415-346-4020

May's Coffee Shop resembles a noodle stand in downtown Tokyo. Set in a skylight filled atrium of the Japantown Center, May's is a tranquil community meeting point for young and old. Bordered by a French pastry shop, a seller of Sanrio goods, an import record store, and a Koi pond, May's has a view of the diversity of this neighborhood. You can order American fare such as Super Burgers or a Grilled Cheese, as well as traditional Japanese favorites like Oyako Donburi (chicken & rice with egg) or Green Tea Ice Cream.

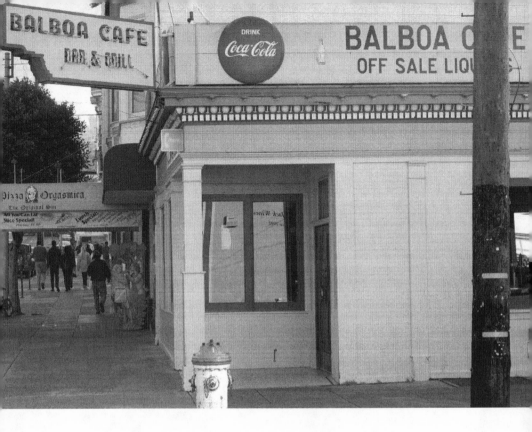

Balboa Cafe

3199 Fillmore Street   San Francisco   415-921-3944

The kitschy outside looks like an old soda shop and the inside like a version of Chicago in the Roaring Twenties, and it's therefore no surprise that the Balboa Cafe is a San Francisco spot where the well-to-do and well-connected come to meet and eat. Co-owned by the Getty family and popular young San Francisco mayor Gavin Newsom, the Balboa has seen many celebrity faces over the years. Opened in 1914, the Balboa's present management team has taken great pains to ensure that it maintains its charm and appeal, both in design and in service. The wood is always polished, the windows perennially clean, and the food reflects a taste for elegance without pretentiousness, which is exactly how to describe the clientele.

The Balboa is an inviting place where a person with a certain polish and aspirations can meet someone who will really appreciate their assets.

Neither marital status nor age are important here, the Balboa expects that everyone will be around as long as it has been, which is why you can order a seared Ahi with truffles and a Muscovy of Duck Confit, or simply grab a Balboa Burger on either a round bun or a baguette. What is important is that the food is to your liking, the company to your interest, and that you will be back again over the next twenty years. Of course, this being a festive meeting place means that drinks are equally important, and at times the Balboa patrons appear to be still in the process of celebrating the repeal of Prohibition. As the Balboa management confirms, "On any given day -- for lunch, brunch, cocktails, or dinner -- couples, singles, old-timers and newcomers can be found reveling in the joyful din of this San Francisco icon."

The Grove

2250 Chestnut Street   San Francisco   415-474-4843

The Grove is in many ways a true distillation of the new Marina neighborhood. After the 1989 Loma Prieta earthquake, which devastated the neighborhood and closed several businesses, the traditionally slow-paced, Italian and Irish Marina gave way to a faster set of young professionals, movers, shakers, and basic fitness buffs. A sunny haven for those who look good and feel good about themselves, the Marina has often been referred to as "the land of milk and honey." The Grove therefore, with it's rustic cabin feel complete with wide-planked barn floors, is a perfect location to absorb the implications of the good life. Much of it is about relaxation, with a bit of work smattered in between.

The cafe itself is built in a lovingly restored Art Deco-style building. Our advice: Order at the counter, sit down in a chair and enjoy some real comfort food. The soups and sandwiches are always good, as are the hot dishes. Read the newspaper and drink a big latte in the morning, an herbal tea in the afternoon, and a glass of wine in the evening. Best of all, bring your dog.

Warming Hut Cafe

Presidio Building 983, Crissy Field   San Francisco   415-561-3042

Located at the bay's edge of the Presidio between the Golden Gate Bridge and the Palace of Fine Arts, Crissy Field has been through many changes over the last century. First it went from shellfish-rich natural wetland to military airstrip, then to barracks-laden military base, then to deserted weed-infested jogging path and launch pad for windsurfing, and now after several years, much civic activism, and $34 million dollars, it has been restored to a balanced version of its original state.

The ecosystem has been reconstituted, the sand has been cleaned, and bikers, runners, kite-flyers, and families with picnics are the new users for this property. Sitting at the Golden Gate Bridge end is the Warming Hut Cafe & Bookstore, an old mine storage building completely converted to modern service using state-of-the-art sustainable practices. The insulation is made of recycled blue jeans, the furniture from salvaged wood, and the cuisine from a variety of organic fair-trade foods inspired by Chez Panisse's star chef, Alice Waters.

It's a good place to stop when out enjoying the day in Crissy Field, at the beach, or on the bridge, but we've found that it is also a good place to go when the day is nice and that's all you need - unless you include one of the most beautiful views in town.

La Terrasse

215 Lincoln   San Francisco   415-922-3463

La Terrasse is one of those fortunate establishments that has been able to find an available location in the Presidio and turn it into a French-influenced bistrot. The interior has high wooden ceilings based on the building's original design from when the Presidio was a major military base. Now however it is an historic national park, as well as a quiet residential neighborhood that also just happens to house the offices of Star Wars filmmaker George Lucas.

Aside from the pedigree of the area, La Terrasse has unobstructed views of the waters of the Bay and beyond. On a clear day you can see parts of the East and North Bay.

The food is warm and comforting, and favorites include the French onion soup gratinee, as well as just about anything with chicken or fish. Wine is both French and Californian, plus you can enjoy them during lunch, brunch or dinner.

The outdoor terrace gets heavy use during nice weather, and is outfitted with wind breakers and heaters to make it a very comfortable spot to meet, eat, or take a date.

Above: The inside of the Blue Danube Coffee House on Clement street

Presidio Heights The Sunset & Richmond Districts

The Inner Sunset and Outer Sunset districts were first established in 1887 by developer Aurelius E. Buckingham, during a time when they were little more than blowing sand dunes and dinky dairy farms far from the lights of the city. Only after Golden Gate Park was created were these areas seriously considered as habitable, but it took the boom years following World War II for their full scale colonization to take place. These neighborhoods remain among the most residential in San Francisco, and like other communities in the city they have their own small town centers. The most prominent and active of these is at the pivotal intersection of 9th Avenue and Irving Street, a venue conveniently located next to the bustling south entrance of popular Golden Gate Park.

Velo Rouge

798 Arguello   San Francisco   415-752-7799

Sometimes a hole in a tree can be a great cafe, but there's nothing I like more than one with an intriguing concept. The Velo Rouge Cafe intrigues me. "Velo" means "bike" in French. "Rouge" means "red." Together they mean "red bicycle," which is what is hanging from the front doorway of the cafe. Concept #1 therefore is: "Don't miss this cafe." I like it.

I also like another concept, which is that they really try to make this place a destination for both locals and people heading to Golden Gate Park. One way they do this is by making it very bike-friendly. A second is by giving you a sun-exposed place to sit outside to eat and drink.

Speaking of eating, the third great concept is the one where the Velo Rouge allows various chefs to cook a dinner menu on a certain night of the week. These are real treats, and over time the chefs and dinners have changed, making this a stop on the entire "underground restaurant" scene, though it is actually licensed to serve food... darn good food, too.

Rigolo

3465 California   San Francisco   415-876-7777

Rigolo means "funny" or "comical" in French, and is a play on words with the name of one of the cafe's concept creators, local patisserie mogul Pascal Rigo, owner of the Boulange de Polk and other locations. Pascal does not own Rigolo, but he does supply fantastic French pastries to this neighborhood cafe in the Laurel Village center, bordering upscale Presidio Heights, booming lower Pacific Heights, and the trendy Inner Richmond.

Rigolo serves various types of people throughout the day: commuters on their way to work looking for coffee and a croissant, stay-at-home mothers doing lunch, and families and singles at the end of the day looking for wine and dinner. In this way its French roots show, because it certainly plays a very integral role in the life of this community. The staff is friendly and attentive, and have a tendency to remember regular customers' usual orders, a very charming ingredient not listed on the menu.

127

Nani's Cafe

2739 Geary   San Francisco   415-928-8817

Nani's Cafe is one of the most pleasant little cafes in San Francisco. It is also one of the hardest to find, kind of like the mythical "Flying Dutchman" of cafes (as in, "Didn't I see it right here the last time? Where could it have gone?"). Located on Geary Street near Masonic, because of its unique location next to a bridge and tunnel a person could drive by it a thousand times and never notice Nani's. But walking by the cafe is a different story. Then it is very hard to ignore. A greenhouse-type covering fronting the lower level of a Victorian in the middle of the city tends to get one noticed.

Inside Nani's is comfortable and calm, almost as if you've been invited into someone's living room. The people behind the counter seem genuinely happy that you've come, and the cafe patrons seem to be genuinely at home, though a bit surprised that someone else has discovered their cool little secret.

Java Beach

1396 La Playa Street   San Francisco   415-665-5282

Whether you're hanging out at Ocean Beach or simply live in the neighborhood, Java Beach is where you want to go. Facing the large sand dunes bordering the water's edge, Java Beach has the '60's retro-appeal of an old Frankie & Annette movie. The café is painted in glossy sunset reds and sunrise yellows, with rich dark wood ceilings accented by fans. Arched doorways separate the counter and entrance from the actual seating area.

Java Beach serves standard San Francisco café beverages, including coffee, tea, herbal tea, healthy cookies, wine, and sandwiches. Patrons love to sit on the front patio for unobstructed access to a possible tan, or on foggy days to roll into the comfortable couches and chairs set near two large windows.

Though Java Beach has a theme, it avoids being a theme café, resisting the urge to sprinkle surfing icons throughout. One of the many ironies of surfing in Northern California is that in order to get the most massive waves you have to have massive weather, including lots of rain and high winds. This means that the crowd varies depending on the forecast. Most come from the neighborhood, and are low-key, mellow, and of all ages. When the surf's up, expect to see a younger, leaner crowd, dressed primarily in the ubiquitous insulated wetsuit that allow "shredding" waves in Northern California to be some of the world's best surfing.

San Francisco Public Cafes

San Francisco is a fascinating, endearing and energizing city. But even the most active traveler has to stop and take it all in from time to time. San Francisco's cafe's are perfect for that. Whether it's an espresso shop in North Beach, a java joint South of Market or an exotic tea blender on Clement Street, San Francisco's cafes are as unique and inviting as the City itself.

John Marks, San Francisco Convention & Visitors Bureau

Leaping Lemur Cafe

San Francisco Zoo, 1 Zoo Road   San Francisco   415-753-7080

The San Francisco Zoo is a busy place, and not just because it's filled with exotic animals and endangered species. The Zoological Society has completed a number of major renovations, including the Leaping Lemur Cafe, making the zoo a great place for family outings, meditative walks, educational trips, and romantic dates.

The cafe was designed in the same circular style as the adjacent antique Dentzel Carousel building, with a high ceiling and large windows to allow diners to gaze at the flamingos just across the way. It is located in the center of the Zoo, just off of Zoo Street and adjacent to the Primate Discovery Center, Flamingo Lake and the new Lemur Forest habitat. The centerpieces of the habitat are the lemur activity towers, where you can help with the operation of the exhibit, hoisting food into the towers. The lemurs will climb up to retrieve the food. You'll also be able to see the animals at their own level in the trees, close enough to observe animal staff weighing or feeding the animals.

The Leaping Lemur Cafe seats up to 250 people and serves a variety of food items, including coffee, pasta, pizza, sandwiches, salads, fish n' chips, burritos and sushi. This innovative menu sates the hunger of many a wild thing.

San Francisco Art Institute Cafe

800 Chestnut Street   San Francisco   415-771-7020

If you want coffee with a view, try the San Francisco Art Institute cafe. Located on the campus of the institute, this cafe serves java along with a variety of visual stimuli. The windows overlook North Beach and the waters of San Francisco Bay. The artwork and architecture that you may pass while entering provide intellectual distraction. Plus, there are the students, a point of origin for many diverse styles, fashions, philosophies, and disciplines. Since its founding in 1871, part of the Institute's mission has been to promote artistic and intellectual freedom, imagination, creativity, experimentation, and risk-taking in a diverse and heterogeneous environment. For over 130 years it has been a meeting ground that has enabled San Francisco Bay Area artists to develop distinct and powerful forms of art.

De Young Museum Cafe

50 Tea Garden Dr   San Francisco   415-750-2614

The De Young Museum is one of San Francisco's cultural treasures, located in Golden Gate Park directly across from another one, the California Academy of Science. Both of these icons have included cafes in their designs, for good reason. People who live in San Francisco love to eat good, healthy, well-prepared food as a highlight of almost any experience. They naturally assume anyone who comes to visit the city is going to feel the same way.

The De Young was founded in 1895, but was rebuilt and reopened in 2005 to international fanfare. The design by Swiss architecture firm Herzog & de Meuron and Fong & Chan Architects in San Francisco combines elements of natural landscaping, organic evolution (the aging metal facade will change color), and pure inspiration. The museum itself contains collections of American art from 17th to 20th centuries, plus from historic Native Americans, Africans and the Pacific.

The cafe interior is very stylish and mod in concept, while the exterior is placed alongside an art-strewn garden courtyard.

The East Bay &
The South Bay

I think people go to cafes to be around other people. Anyone can make coffee at home, often as good as or better than what the cafes serve. So I think it's just a desire to be around people, whether to observe or interact.
The venerable cafe scene of Berkeley, California, predates the java craze of both Los Angeles and Seattle...You can't swing a Marxist or throw a Birkenstock without hitting a cafe in Berkeley and the surrounding area

Chris Rubin
TRAVEL + LEISURE Magazine

The San Francisco Bay Area is unique in that it has not one but three major cities within its borders. Each of these cities occupies a point on a triangle: San Francisco, San Jose in the South Bay, and Oakland in the East Bay. Oakland has traditionally been a major port for trade with the Far East, and has often felt overshadowed by flashier San Francisco. But Oakland, along with its intellectual partner Berkeley, has had its own cafe society for quite a while. Berkeley (and its University) in particular has cultivated its cafes into being recognized forces for social change, and over the last fifty years this role has been visible time after time.

Presently Berkeley's cafes are stretching their wings and expanding their offerings. Cafes such as the venerable Poulet, Alice Water's Cafe Fanny, and sleek Cafe Rouge provide gourmet-level cuisine in a laid-back setting.

The South Bay is anchored by the Silicon Valley technology culture, and metros such as San Jose and Palo Alto. Palo Alto hosts Stanford University, a preeminent cultural and economic force in the region. In local towns ranging from Saratoga, Los Altos, Sunnyvale and Redwood City, to Menlo Park, San Mateo, San Carlos and Burlingame, the sunshine oriented cafe culture of the South Bay and the Peninsula has much to admire.

Above: Poulet in Berkeley
Above Top: Left Bank, Menlo Park

Peet's Coffee & Tea

2124 Vine Street   Berkeley   510-841-0564

If you are very observant you will notice it right away. If you're just average it may take awhile. Either way, it soon becomes apparent that Peet's has high aspirations. Of course they include providing superb coffee and tea to devoted customers, but they also include objectives such as fair-trade suppliers, sustainable farming, recycling food wastes, and healthcare in coffee-growing communities. Perhaps it is for all of these reasons that Peet's has an extremely loyal and satisfied following.

"With age comes wisdom and responsibility." Peet's has been around since P.S. time (pre-Starbucks). The first Peet's was opened in Berkeley by Alfred Peet in 1966. The superior quality of his blends and the skill of his deep roast methods eventually lead to Peet's being referred to as 'the grandfather of specialty coffee.' You can see the inherent appreciation of cafe culture in the layout of each Peet's cafe and in the attitude of the clientele. Nowhere is this more evident than at the location where Peet's Coffee was born. Peet's on Vine Street in Berkeley is both old and modern.

Granite walls, dark tiles, and a streamlined design do not scream 1960's, but the attitude of the customers and the staff does. Everyone is friendly, everyone is calm, everyone is at peace. The atmosphere has an almost religious tone, as if each person realizes that this is 'where it all began.' The aura is enhanced not only by the variety of beans, blends, tea, and educational literature available, but also by the vast collection of antiques and accessories. Gaggia espresso machines sit next to Livia 90's, while coffee mugs run the gamut from Babar to Beehouse. Circumnavigating the cafe is a shelf holding an extensive museum-quality display of antique measuring scales, below which are vintage cafe posters from Belgium and France. Other Peet's locations reflect these themes, and also work to accentuate the existing architecture (see photos next page, San Francisco's Peet's on Fillmore - top, and Peet's on Polk - bottom right). But of course what's important is that people love the coffee.

Cafe La Tartine

830 Middlefield   Redwood City   650-474-2233

Cafe La Tartine is situated in one of the renovated districts of downtown Redwood City, across from the movie theater, other restaurants, a concert hall, and the historical society. The street is lined with high palm trees, and the natural lighting in this part of the Bay Area is pleasant and a bit Mediterranean. This is fortunate, because there is plenty of outdoor seating at La Tartine.

The interior of the cafe is spacious and comfortable, with many windows to allow natural light inside, as well as plenty of tables and chairs for eating or reading. The highlight of the cafe, however, is not its design, but its pastry and food selections. These range from tarts and chocolates and cookies to sandwiches and savory dishes. Of course, wine and coffee and other beverages are on hand to wash it all down. A friendly and attractive staff completes the tableau.

Cafe Borrone

1010 El Camino Real   Menlo Park   650-327-0830

Cafe Borrone is located on El Camino Real in Menlo Park, which when one is driving by just looks like a little spot where people grab a quick lunch next to a popular local bookstore. The truth is, Cafe Borrone is a destination cafe. You walk out of your door, look at the blue sky, decide you want a delicious sandwich, panini, crepe, wine or soda, then head there directly. This is true whether you live in San Jose or in San Francisco. Cafe Borrone is a great place to be.

The reasons are simple: the food is good, the prices are fair, the drinks are right, and the ambiance is like a mini-vacation. You can sit and read the newspaper, international magazines, or a book. You can work on your computer, with the sounds of the fountain in the background. You can people-watch. People watching is very entertaining, because Cafe Borrone attracts a wide range of types from up and down the Peninsula: Intellectuals, techies, oldsters, youngsters, style hounds and fashionistas, foreigners and natives. As long as you have a seat, and a cool beverage on a warm day, you have a day's worth of stimulation.

Strolling the South Bay

Clockwise from top left (opposite page): Bistro Vida (Menlo Park), Bistro Vida, Bistro Vida , The Left Bank Brasserie (Menlo Park), The Left Bank Brasserie, Pamplemousse (Redwood City)

The North Bay:
Marin &
Napa / Sonoma

Marin County is located in what is locally referred to as the North Bay, the land north of San Francisco across Golden Gate Bridge. The area has a beautiful landscape, gifted with cliffs and beaches, islands and forests. One such forest is the California Redwood reserve known as Muir Woods, a good spot for a hike. The woods are a tangible part of the history of this region, and its ancient trees are unique to Northern California. Towering over Muir Woods and most of Marin is the evergreen peak of Mount Tamalpais, another excellent location for hiking and biking. At the base of Mount "Tam" sit the towns of San Anselmo, San Raphael, Larkspur, and Mill Valley. Each are home to a number of interesting cafes.

A mere forty minutes north of Marin are the Napa and Sonoma valleys, America's premier wine growing regions. It is the proximity of these valleys that has contributed greatly to both the ingrained appreciation of wine by San Franciscans, and to its cafe culture's second greatest source of inspiration.

Above: The serene garden courtyard of the Sunflower Cafe in downtown Sonoma

The Depot Bookstore & Café

87 Throckmorton Avenue   Mill Valley   415-383-2665

A favorite of residents and tourists alike, the Depot is a converted trolley station in the center of town. Formerly used as a transit point for nature lovers taking trams to the top of nearby Mount Tamalpais, the building looks much as at did in the earlier part of the 20th century. Adjacent to the town square, the bookstore has a varied and rather erudite selection for its petite size, reflecting not only the quality of the management but also customer tastes. The cafe has a very well-run kitchen with large gourmet sandwiches such as Grilled Cheese with Black Forest Ham, as well as attractive indoor and outdoor seating. The outdoor seating in particular can be considered some of the best and sunniest in the North Bay, with a nice amount of people watching available. This is a great place to go when you are in San Francisco on one of its cloudier days and seriously need to find some ultraviolets, a Torani soda, and a travel magazine.

Emporio Rulli

464 Magnolia Avenue   Larkspur   415-924-7478

Whenever I enter Emporio Rulli and stand on its rich marble-tiled floors, gazing past the original mural by Carlo Marchiori, I catch myself thinking, "Rome wasn't built in a day, but this is a nice start." Emporio Rulli supplies enough sensation to fill an entire palazzo. Crystal chandeliers hang overhead, illuminating a wealth of pastries, candies, panini, chocolates, biscotti, tortas, focaccia, gelato, and panforte. There are more choices here than you could possible eat in a day, though some customers at the tables seem intent to give it a try. The Italian glass pastry case stretches from one end of the room to the next, interrupted only by doors leading to what used to be two other separate stores. Like Caesar before him, Rulli has annexed and expanded in order to meet the needs of his public.

After learning his craft from master bakers in northern Italy, Rulli returned to the United States and with his wife, Jeannie, opened their first shop in 1988. At that time the Rulli name was not well known, but as customers came to sample the goods and then returned with friends, the Rulli mystique grew. Over the years the single pasticceria, or pastry shop, has evolved to include in its description both "gelateria" and "torrefazione," as well as wine shop.

One aspect of Rulli's technique that may be missed by the average customer, even while they are appreciating every morsel of his creations, is his range. As observed by Corby Kummer in the Atlantic Monthly magazine, "...a shop that make its own panettone, for instance, as many pastry shops around Milan and Turin do, will not always offer it year-round, as Rulli does, and will seldom offer for breakfast, alongside toasted wedges of panettone, the Florentine specialty budino di riso...[Rulli has] the specialties of many Italian regions polished up and presented all together." I only have three things to say to that: Magare (to wish), Mangiare (to eat), and Grazie Mille!

BookBeat

28 Bolinas Rd   Fairfax   415-256-9060

Fairfax is known as a "hippie haven," while at the same time having some pretty upscale home values. The town seems to have reconciled both aspects of its personality with what appears to be more per capita cafes and new age stores than anywhere else in Marin.

A very unique cafe in town is BookBeat, which combines a cafe and bookshop to create a literary coffeehouse. High ceilings let plenty of light illuminate the many local and national selections they carry, including some that are very particular to the region.

Music is on tap on certain nights, and you can tell by the number of event flyers at its front door that if you're looking for something to do, or a place to launch a literary revolution, this is it.

Fairfax Coffee Roastery

4 Bolinas Rd   Fairfax   415-256-1373

Situated on the corner of one of Fairfax's few main intersections, this cafe lures you inside with the promise of freshly roasted coffee, then keeps you from leaving by enticing you with its Art Nouveau designs, curving marble countertop, generous seating, cute staff, and decidedly well-planned menu. Who can escape the temptation of a marshmallow ripple cocoa, or a Torani-based Italian soda?

If you're in the market for vegetarian or vegan dishes, or even what are labeled as "Grandma's cookies," you've come to the right cafe. If you just happen to want to meet a friend, work on your computer, or write a novel, that's good too. On the other hand, if you're an anti-social right-wing grouch, we recommend you move on. There's too much positivity happening here for you.

Aroma Cafe

1122 4th Street   San Rafael   415-459-4340

Aroma Cafe is located in the center of San Raphael, and is therefore one of the busiest cafes in town. It is also next door to the local fine arts movie theater, which makes it very lucky. It gets patrons who are going to or coming from seeing a film, as well as those who just want to sit all day with a cup of java and a muffin. When the summer heat picks up in Marin, this is also a good place to cool off.

The Aroma Cafe is quite long, and because it shares the building with the movie theater, the ceilings are also quite high. In fact, I've been told that if you look up you can see what used to be part of an upper balcony of the movie theater. Unfortunately, I haven't been able to confirm whether that much is true, or just part of some Marin urban legend. Either way, it's a fun story to repeat.

Caffe Acri

1 Main Street   Tiburon   415-435-8515

Caffe Acri's most attractive aspects are its design and its location. The design is that of a modern Italian caffe and gelatoria, with chrome armed chairs, marble table tops and floors, a large counter for viewing pastries, and often the sound of brewing coffee.

The location is on Tiburon's waterfront and corner of Main Street, which means that its cafe tables are like a siren's call to travelers, day trippers, hikers and bikers just off the ferry, and anyone who has ever visited Europe in the summer.

Caffe Acri offers a variety of pastries, paninis and sandwiches, spumoni, cookies, gelato, wine, and hot beverages. Caffe Acri is a good spot for a meeting, a rendez-vous, or to get some afternoon sun.

Sam's Anchor Cafe

27 Main Street   Tiburon   415-435-4527

We love Sam's Cafe, that is, when we can get a seat outdoors. Which is about 75% of time, not a bad average for a place with one of the best views of the Bay, Angel Island, and glorious San Francisco on a sunny day. Going to Sam's is always like a mini-vacation.

Sam's has well prepared food and a good choice of drinks, pleasant service, and choice seats. Of course, it's all about the seats. When you're sitting outside on Sam's deck it is very easy to forget that your chair is literally situated over water, or that San Francisco, which seems so close, is actually 20 minutes away by car.

Birds put things in perspective, as they swoop over the tops of the docked sailboats in the little Tiburon marina in front of the restaurant. If you're one of the fortunate who has your own vessel you can even pull right in for lunch. If you like boats but don't have access to one, the you can still take a ferry from Fisherman's Wharf, then go to Angel Island and build up an appetite with a nice bike excursion.

Inside of the restaurant, Sam's has a tranquil atmosphere, perfect for brunches, romance, family meals, and groups. The food is solid Northern California coastal cuisine: cioppino, steamed clams, oysters, swordfish, salmon, grilled prawns, grilled tofu-vegetable brochette, beer batter onion rings, organic baby spinach salad, and a very long brunch menu.

CAFE CUISINE

One that desires to excel
should endeavor in those
things that are in them-
selves most excellent.

-- Epictetus

Whenever you are sincerely pleased you
are nourished.

-- Ralph Waldo Emerson

The Balboa Cafe Calamari Fritta

Calamari-based dishes are widespread in San Francisco, thanks to its proximity to the sea and the profound influence of Italian cooking. Fried calamari is easier to find as an appetizer or bar snack than peanuts, and only the freshest squid is used. In San Francisco, Calamari Fritta must melt in the mouth like butter, any chewiness being an indication that the main ingredient was frozen before preparation, a practice sure to cast doubt on the talents of the chef. This recipe for Calamari Fritta is from the Balboa Cafe in the Marina.

Clean the squid by cutting off the tentacles and removing the soft exoskeleton and innards with the back of your knife. To do this, hold the top of the squid and with one motion move the knife forward and everything will come out. (Put something in front of the squid or it will splash everywhere) What remains are the tentacles and the clean body of the squid.

Slice the body crosswise into little rings. Do not cut the tentacles. Rinse everything in mesh basket when done.

To bread the squid, combine the breading ingredients in a medium-sized bowl. Mix all together with a fork and place

1 lb very fresh squid

BREADING:
4 cups flour
11/2 cups Japanese bread crumbs (Panko)
1/4 cup corn starch
1 tablespoon salt
1 tablespoon pepper

1 quart Canola oil

the mesh basket containing the squid into the bowl containing the breading mixture. Shake around and sift until all pieces of squid are well coated.

Place the squid into a pot of oil at 350 degrees, cook for 4 minutes or until crispy.

Serve with lemon or your choice of dipping sauce.

The Absinthe Ginger Rogers

This drink is legendary at Absinthe, and is almost as addictive as the brasserie's namesake.

Prepare ginger syrup:
Shave ginger into thin slices. Whisk water and sugar together until sugar is well dissolved. Add ginger slices. Bring to boil on stove, reduce heat to low and let simmer for 4 hours or until mixture has been reduced by 1/4 and ginger is fully candied. Remove from stove and add peppercorns. Let cool naturally to room temperature. Strain and squeeze all excess juice from ginger.

Prepare Ginger Rogers:
Cover mint leaves with ginger syrup. Muddle. Add ice, gin, and juice. Top glass with ginger ale

1 1/2 oz gin
1/2 oz. ginger syrup
1/2 oz. lemon/lime juice
Ginger ale (varies by glass size)
6 fresh mint leaves (mint sprig)

Ginger Syrup:
1 lb ginger
4 quarts sugar
6 black peppercorns
6 quarts water

Portobello & Onion Risotto

Courtesy of Café Andre, this dish always results in demands for second helpings.

Heat a wide saucepan over a medium-high flame, then add the olive oil to coat the bottom of the pan. Add the onions, garlic, 3/4 of the mushrooms, paprika and oregano, and cook until the onion is translucent.

Add the arborio rice and stir frequently to coat with the oil. Cook for 2-3 minutes. Add white wine or white wine vinegar and stir.

When the wine is absorbed into the rice add 1/2 cup of chicken stock. When the stock is absorbed into rice, repeat the process four times, using four equal amounts of stock. Keep the rice at medium to medium-high while stirring either continually or at least 5 times per minute.

3 Portobello mushrooms wiped with a damp cloth and chopped into medium pieces. Do not rinse under water
3 tablespoons olive oil
3 1/2 cups chicken stock
2 onions, chopped
1 1/2 cups Arborio rice
3/4 cup white wine or white wine vinegar
2 cloves garlic, minced or chopped
1/2 teaspoon of oregano
1/2 teaspoon of paprika
salt & pepper to taste
1/4 ounce butter
1/4 cup grated Parmesan

After the addition of the second equal amount of stock add the rest of the mushrooms. After the addition of the final amount of stock, when the liquid is absorbed and the rice is cooked, adjust seasonings with salt and pepper, then fold in the butter and parmesan, and remove from heat.

Gruyére & Cheddar Cheese and Macaroni

Café Andre's take on Macaroni and Cheese, a variation of a well-known three-cheese recipe for this comfort food.

Pasta:
Pre-heat oven to 350 degrees. Cook pasta in a pot of boiling water until al dente. Do not overcook. Drain.

Sauce:
Melt butter in sauce pan over medium heat. When butter is completely melted and begins to bubble, add flour. Stir 2-3 minutes over medium flame so that mixture forms a tan-colored creamy paste. Add milk to mixture, stirring over medium heat for 3-4 minutes. Add spices, stir in onions and cheeses, cook for 2 minutes.

1/2 lb macaroni pasta shells (elbows)
2 3/4 cup milk
1/2 stick unsalted butter
1/4 cup flour
1 teaspoon salt
1/8 teaspoon pepper
1/8 teaspoon ginger
1/8 teaspoon cinnamon
1/8 teaspoon cayenne pepper
3 cups grated white cheddar (over 8+ oz)
1 cup grated gruyere cheese (over 4+ oz)
1 1/2 chopped onions

Bake:
Place drained pasta in an oven-proof casserole pan. Pour cheese-onion sauce over pasta. Mix thoroughly, spreading sauce and pasta mixture evenly in pan. Place casserole in oven for 12 minutes.

CAFE RESOURCES

Coffee & Tea

Caffe Roma Coffee Roasting Company
885 Bryant
San Francisco, CA
415-296-7662
www.cafferoma.com

Caffe Trieste
609 Vallejo
San Francisco, CA 94133
415-550-1107
www.caffetrieste.com

David Rio Coffee & Tea, Inc.
PO Box 885462
San Francisco, CA 94188
800-454-9605
www.davidrio.com

Graffeo Coffee Roasting Company
735 Columbus Avenue
San Francisco, CA 94133
415-986-2420

Martha's & Brothers Coffee Company
745 Cortland Avenue
San Francisco, CA
415-642-7585

Mr. Espresso
696 3rd
Oakland, CA 94607
510-287-5200

Peaberry's Coffee and Tea
4059 Emery Street
Emeryville, CA 94608
510-420-0473

Peet's Coffee & Tea
PO Box 12509
Berkeley, CA 94712-3509
800-999-2132
www.peets.com
mailorder@peets.com

Republic of Tea
8 Digital Drive, Suite 100
Novato, CA 94949
1-800-298-4832
www.republicoftea.com

Chocolate & Cocoa

Ghirardelli Chocolate Shop & Caffe
900 North Point Street, Box 142
West Plaza of Ghirardelli Square
San Francisco
415-474-1414

Local tea producer **David Rio** is an excellent example of Bay Area sensibilities. Blending eastern traditions with western style, David Rio is an innovative tea company that brings eclectic blends, diverse flavors and classic style to each of its unique tea products. Two of its main product lines are chai and tea. The chai comes in a variety of flavors, such as POWER Chai, Chocolate Chai Cooler, Tiger Spice Chai, Chocolate Chimp Chai, Tortoise Green Tea Chai, Elephant Vanilla Chai, Orca Spice Sugar Free Chai, and Giraffe Decaf Chai. Many of the Chai products are named after animals, and David Rio supports animal organizations such as Cat Tales (an endangered species rescue organization), the Humane Society and Amazing Greys - Retired Racers.

David Rio also offers a line of distinctive, fine loose leaf teas which focus on green teas and unique Japanese teas. We think that the design of the tea tins is especially attractive. Tea blends include Japanese Breakfast, Dragon Phoenix Pearls, La France Pear, Fuji Apple, Tahitian Tangerine, Genmaicha, Twin Peaks Tisane, Green Passion, Edible Green Tea, and Hatsu Mukashi Matcha. Caffeine-free Buddha's choice is made of toasted Buckwheat – a staple in Japanese beverage culture. On June 6, 2002 The San Francisco Mayor's Committee for the Employment of People with Disabilities named David Rio "Employer of the Year". David Rio was chosen for its commitment in hiring people with disabilities. 800-454-9605, www.davidrio.com

Torani flavored syrups are a part of San Francisco's cafe heritage. In 1925, husband and wife team Rinaldo and Ezilda Torre began blending Italian syrups from heirloom recipes that Rinaldo had brought from Lucca, Italy. The pair soon perfected five flavors - Anisette, Grenadine, Lemon, Orgeat (almond) and Tamarindo - and shared them with their neighbors throughout North Beach, San Francisco's flourishing Italian community. Mixed with soda water, the syrups were instantly a local favorite, and café owners in America were introduced to the "Italian Soda." The R. Torre & Company was born, and a line of authentic Italian syrups emerged, under the brand name "Torani."

Over the next sixty years, Torani grew into a nationally recognized brand. Then, in the 1980's, coffee industry veteran "Brandy" Brandenburger noticed the brightly colored Torani bottles while visiting San Francisco's landmark café, Caffé Trieste. Experimenting with various blends, he added a shot of Torani to an espresso drink, hoping the flavor might lend a new appeal to the traditional beverage. With this mixture Brandenburger created and introduced the novel concept of the flavored caffe latte. Soon coffee lovers everywhere were requesting Torani-flavored espresso drinks and a new American classic was born. The rest is history. For decades,

Torani's red, gold and blue labels have been a part of the cafe lifestyle. Much has changed over the years, but Torani is still family-owned and -operated in South San Francisco, not far from its North Beach origins. Torani now exports over 70 syrup flavors across the country and around the world and continues to offer new ways to add flavor and originality to beverages and culinary pursuits.

Consumers can purchase Torani at select grocery stores, specialty retailers and through online distributors. Cafes can purchase Torani products through their distributor or by contacting Torani directly for more information. Go to www.torani.com, or call 800-775-1925.

Guittard Chocolate Company
10 Guittard Road
Burlingame, CA
800-468-2462

XOX Truffles
754 Columbus Avenue
San Francisco, CA
415-421-4814

Cafe Decor, Design & BAR

Cafe Society
San Francisco, CA
415.305.8381
www.cafesocietystore.com
(Cafe Decor & Antiques)

Music

Putumayo World Music
324 Lafayette Street, 7th Floor
New York, NY 10012
1-888 PUTUMAYO (788-8629)
1-800-995-9588 ext. 226 (for Cafes & Retailers)
www.putumayo.com

Cafe del Mar, Version 5
MCA Records
(Various Outlets)

Cafe Tours

Mangia! North Beach Tour with GraceAnn Walden
415-397-8530

Gourmet Walks
www.GourmetWalks.com

For modern cafe and kitchen items for the home, *Zinc Details* is one of several fantastic San Francisco Bay Area stores. Founded in 1990, Zinc Details' collection includes Bee House teapots, Uten Silo boards, Stelton Salt & Pepper sets, and Alessi Espresso Makers. Clean without being sterile, colorful without being cluttered, the collection of national and international classics takes its cue from the best of Japan and Scandinavia and dovetails brilliantly with the store's own line of dinnerware, lighting and other accessories. They have also added a store within a store for the work of internationally celebrated potter and textile designer, Jonathan Adler. The firm has two locations, one at 1905 Fillmore in San Francisco, and one nearby on California Street. www.zincdetails.com, 415-776-2100

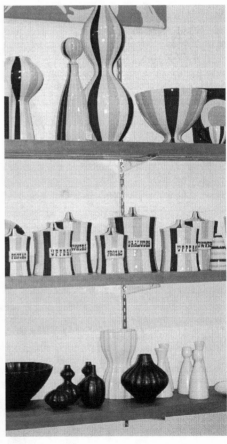